A Survival Guide to the Portuguese Camino in Galicia

By Jeffery Barrera

Text copyright © 2024 Jeffery Barrera (**eleventh edition**)

First edition © 2014 Jeffery Barrera

All Rights Reserved

All diagrams and maps © Jeffery Barrera

All photographs © of Fresco Tours & Jeffery Barrera

Cover art © Jeffery Barrera

ISBN-13: 978-1983736780

ISBN-10: 1983736783

I appreciate any and all feedback, comments and corrections.

Please do not hesitate to contact me at:
Jeffery@barrerabooks.com
www.barrerabooks.com
or
Share a **review** at **Amazon.com**
or
Even like and/or follow **A Survival Guide to the Camino** on **Facebook, Instagram** and/or **X (Twitter)**
for regular updates from the Camino

for Ana, my compass and sextant

Santiago de Galiza,
Longe fica o vosso altar:
Peregrino que lá chegue
Não sabe se há-de voltar.

Santiago of Galicia
Your altar is far
Pilgrim that arrives there
Knows not if he will return

(from the Miragaia Romance)

Table of Contents

Preface _____ 9

Introduction _____ 13
Popular saying - Aymeric Picaud and his Codex Calixtinus - Locals ignoring you - 1993 - Coffee in Spain - The Scallop Shell - Menú del Día (Menu of the Day) - The conspiracy theory: Bishop Priscillian – Hieronymus Münzer and his travels through Spain and Portugal – León of Rosmithal and his travels through Europe – Giovanni Battista Confalonieri and his pilgrimage to Santiago

Timeline of the pilgrimage site _____ 35

Map Legend _____ 37

Stage 1 Map _____ 38

Stage 1. Tui to Porriño (+16 km) _____ 39
The International Bridge - Alfonso IX - Mount Aloia - King Witiza - The Aloia mares - San Telmo (Saint Elmo), the saint who is not a saint - Local artist Xai Óscar and his art - As Gándaras Industrial Estate in Porriño

Stage 2 Map _____ 54

Stage 2. Porriño to Redondela (+14.5 km) _____ 55
As Gándaras de Budiño - Antonio Palacios - Albariño wine country (and Spanish wine in general) - Cruceiros - The poet of Mos - Santa Eulalia (Saint Eulalia) - The Irmandiños (the fraternity or brotherhood)

Stage 3 Map _____ 64

Stage 3. Redondela to Pontevedra (20 km) _____ 65
The viaducts - Xan Carallás - La Coca - San Simón Island - Battle of Rande - Castle of Soutomaior and Pedro Madruga - Battle of Pontesampaio - Santa Marta

Stage 4 Map _____ 76

Stage 4. Pontevedra to Caldas de Reis (23.7 km) _____ 77
Teucrus - Santa Clara's eggs - Little John or Sister María? - Paio Gómez Chariño - The Feast of Santiaguiño do Burgo - Don't mess with the locals - Variante Espiritual (The Alternative Spiritual Route) - Saint Amaro, Amarus, Mauro or Maurus - Alfonso II the Chaste - Towns and Parroquias - Aguardiente - Queimada

Stage 5 Map   90

Stage 5. Caldas de Reis to Padrón (18.5 km)   91

Ugly Spanish towns - Santa Mariña (Saint Marina) - The battle at Casal do Erigio - La Bella Otero (The Beautiful or 'Belle' Otero) - The Order of Santiago - Herbón - The Spanish Civil War in Galicia

Stage 6 Map   102

Stage 6. Padrón to Santiago de Compostela (23.5 km)   103

Padrón Peppers - The surprising literary heritage of Padrón - Clubs - Queen Lupa's Castle - A 10.000.000 euros (or more) theft - Statue of the 'Dos Marías' (Two Marys)

Santiago de Compostela   117

Santiago, UNESCO World Heritage Site – The Fountain do Franco on Rúa do Franco - Pilgrim rites - Indulgences - Santiago el Mayor (St. James the Greater) - The Virgin Mary and St. James - Legend of the remains and burial of Santiago - Legend of the battle of Clavijo - Tribute of the 100 maidens - Abastos market - Gin and tonics in Galicia (and Spain)

Annex I. Valença do Minho   135

San Teotonio (Saint Theotonius) - The Rooster of Barcelos

Annex II – General Spanish Etiquette   141

Annex III - Accommodation   145

Preface

Please note that if you have bought 'A Survival Guide to the Camino de Santiago in Galicia', which covers the French route to Santiago, you will find that some sections and entries in this guidebook are similar or even the same. Although this guidebook has been researched, written and edited specifically for the Portuguese route, there are general (and specific) aspects of Galicia and the Camino that are common to both the French and the Portuguese routes.

In 2019, all of the milestones along the Portuguese Camino were replaced and the Camino became slightly longer. C'est la vie!

Most likely, if you have decided to walk the Portuguese Camino, you have either already walked the French Camino, or you have decided to avoid the crowds on the French Camino. In either case, you will be walking a completely *different* Camino from the much more popular French route.

Likewise, you may also have already started to research and compile information about the Portuguese Camino. And you have probably already discovered that, whereas there are dozens (hundreds) of guidebooks available for the classic French Camino, there is just a handful for the Portuguese Camino. Indeed, even the wealth of information available online when it comes to the French Camino dwindles down to a trickle when researching the Portuguese Camino.

In Spain we have a saying that roughly translates as: *comparisons are odious*. Unfortunately, when it comes to the Portuguese Camino, comparisons with the French Camino appear to be inevitable. Some are much more evident than others, such as walking north instead of chasing the sun, or walking longer stretches alone and having to use the bushes more often due to the lack of pilgrim services. On the other hand, the Portuguese Camino will also take you through Galicia's most renowned wine region and by all of the most important Camino related sights in Galicia. It will also take you along the most important Roman Road in this part of the Iberian Peninsula, which linked (current) Portugal with Galicia and Castile.

Furthermore, perhaps the highlight of the Portuguese Camino is that you will have the opportunity to actually *walk* in the footsteps of the

Apostle Saint James and visit the place where in life he carried out his ministry in Spain. If Santiago de Compostela is the place where pilgrims have venerated for centuries the death of Saint James, the town of Padrón is where pilgrims can celebrate the life of the Apostle and see *where it all began*.

A Survival Guide to the Portuguese Camino in Galicia will not only provide you with simple, concise and to-the-point information about the route you are following, but will also help you understand and appreciate Spanish idiosyncrasy, which is usually the most intriguing, and at times frustrating, part of a trip for travellers.

This is also a guidebook that provides insider insight and information about the Camino; information on where you are walking, why you are looking at things and how to make the most of your experience; all that stuff that is not readily available to travellers from abroad.

In a nutshell, this is a guidebook written by a Spanish pilgrim for pilgrims from abroad.

Please note that this guidebook covers **only** the last section of the Portuguese Camino, **the part that crosses Galicia in Spain**. It does **not** cover any of the stages in Portugal.

All the information in this guidebook was accurate at the time of writing and revision. However, as I have mentioned in previous editions, the Camino is *alive*, and thrives and agonises in line with current events. This year has been another exceptional year. Indeed, every single record regarding pilgrim numbers has been broken, businesses are thriving, and it does not look like in the foreseeable future Camino enthusiasm with dwindle.

As in other editions, if you spot any inaccuracies, please accept my apologies and do not hesitate to contact me.

Finally, although I work as a guide on the Camino, I do not get (or have got) a commission, nor will you get a discount if you show my book at any of the mentioned places (you may get a smile though!). The places I mention are based on my own experience, because I like the places and the people, and because I feel like it! The Camino is much more than beautiful scenery and medieval churches; the Camino is also the people you meet, both other pilgrims and locals. These are the memories you are most likely to remember in the future, and this is why I do not have any second thoughts about including names and businesses, because thanks to these people and their bars, restaurants and hotels, the Camino continues to offer unforgettable experiences to the pilgrim who is just passing through.

This guidebook is organised in six chapters that correspond to the commonly suggested daily stages to be covered on foot. Indeed, most of my stages will coincide with the stages suggested in any other guidebook. In this manner, there are six chapters corresponding to six stages, some stages longer in distance than others. There is also a final chapter for the city of Santiago de Compostela, a general introductory chapter and two annexes, one for the Portuguese town of Valença do Minho, and the other on general Spanish culture.

Each chapter describes a departure town and a town of arrival and is presented with a schematic map of the stage. The kilometres to be covered on each stage are indicated by the departure town. There is also a diagram with the villages, hamlets and other points of interest you will walk through during that stage with kilometre indicators in concordance with the milestones (*kilometrestones*) that mark the route. These milestones indicate the remaining kilometres to Santiago, so in this manner you will always have a rough (or precise) idea of where you are. Remember that although I will use the term milestone, the distances are always expressed in kilometres (roughly, 1 mile corresponds to 1.6 kilometres). The diagram also provides a general elevation profile of the elevation gain and loss throughout the stage.

General information is provided for each village or place of interest as well as information on how to get in and out of the towns (not always the easiest thing). Finally, there are miscellaneous information snippets about the places you are travelling through or near to. This information can be historical, religious, artistic, or anything else related to Spanish and Galician culture and/or customs.

These information snippets are a collection of thoughts and notes I have compiled while on and off the Camino. These have all been researched and crosschecked, although I have not included a reference section, so you will have to take my word for it. I am sure many more can be added (and others perhaps omitted), once again, I am open to any suggestion that you would like to send my way.

I am aware that some people's beliefs may clash with other people's beliefs (especially when talking about religion or politics) and therefore I have made every effort to be respectful with all. I will also ask you in kind to read with an open mind, that the Camino is now a meeting place and a melting pot for people from all walks of life and there is room for everyone as long as we all respect each other.

I would like to conclude this preface with my *Camino mantra* that I believe has helped more than one pilgrim in my groups:

Stop racing; there will always be someone faster (and slower) than you.

Stop worrying about doing it right; every Camino is right, as long as it is yours.

Stop looking for what you came for and you will eventually find it.

Buen camino! (Have a good Camino!)

Jeffery

Madrid and Santiago de Compostela, December 2023. Last Year of the Pandemic.

Introduction

This guidebook covers the last 118 kilometres to Santiago on the Portuguese route, covering the section of the Portuguese Camino in Galicia, starting on the border with Portugal and ending in Santiago de Compostela.

The Portuguese Camino

The popularity of the Portuguese Camino has steadily increased over the last ten years and it is now the second most walked route to Santiago. However, the Portuguese Camino is still far behind the classic French route regarding numbers, accounting for approximately 20% of all the pilgrims in 2019. Or in other words, whereas (around) 190.000 pilgrims walked the French Camino in 2019, just over 70.000 walked the Portuguese Camino. Official figures for this year suggest that the Portuguese Camino will remain the same for 2023.

The implication of this is evident: fewer pilgrims mean fewer services (although this is gradually changing in line with the increase of pilgrims). Furthermore, the popularity of the Portuguese Camino is still a fairly recent phenomenon, which means that there are fewer trails and paths. Indeed, Camino associations are still striving and working hard at altering sections of the Portuguese Camino with the aim of keeping pilgrims off the busy roads and taking them through the more scenic and safer trails. Once again the implication of this is evident: new alternative routes suddenly appear and pilgrims are faced with hard dilemmas as they encounter yellow arrows pointing in opposite directions.

On the other hand, what we do know with perhaps more accuracy than on the French Camino are the towns and villages that the Portuguese Camino goes through. This is thanks to the numerous travellers and pilgrims who followed this route and left written accounts of their journeys. Travellers and pilgrims such as Confalonieri, Münzer and Rosmithal all wrote diaries of their travels through this part of Spain and they all passed through the towns you will be walking through on your pilgrimage. By the late Middle Ages and onwards, the wonders of the Kingdom of Portugal represented an almost obligatory destination for travellers (tourists?) from abroad, and it was not unusual for these same travellers to later follow the *road* north and pay their respects to

Saint James in Santiago de Compostela. The significant overall decline in pilgrims to Santiago during the 18th, 19th and most of the 20th centuries was also felt on the Portuguese Camino to the extent that this route was basically forgotten till the success of the French Camino put the pilgrimage to Santiago back on the map.

The western Galician coast has historically always been the backbone for commerce and trade for the region. Cut off from the rest of Spain by the Mountains of Galicia that form a natural barrier between Galicia and Castile, Galicia has tended in modern times to look southwards, towards Portugal and westwards towards the Atlantic Ocean. Unsurprisingly, Galicia's largest city is the industrial port of Vigo, just off the Portuguese Camino and less than half an hour away from Portugal. Galicia's second largest city is the important harbour and port of A Coruña, an hour north of Santiago. What all of this has meant for modern day pilgrims is the proximity to the Camino of the most important expressways (that link these commercial hubs on the west coast), the largest industrial estates and some of the most populated towns in Galicia.

For your peace of mind, the Portuguese Camino does a good job of avoiding most of the above, and the vast majority of the Camino is on trails, paths and quiet country lanes.

Popular saying about the Camino:

Con pan y vino, se hace el Camino. (With bread and wine you'll be able to walk the Camino).

Note that this popular saying not only draws on the underlying religious meaning the Camino represents for many pilgrims, but perhaps more clearly on two representative staple food items for an average Spaniard at lunch time. Indeed, many 'Menus of Day' include bread and a bottle of House Wine.

Wine country versus dairy country

If someone were to ask me what the most significant difference between the French Camino and the Portuguese Camino is, the answer is simple: you will be walking through wine country instead of dairy country. If you are familiar with the French Camino as it makes its way across Lugo, you will undoubtedly associate your experience with cows, dairy farms and cow pies. None of that exists on the Portuguese Camino as the local agriculture is almost exclusively wine production, which means vineyards, *bodegas* and no cow pies. So, if you are a wine enthusiast (like me), then get prepared for a real treat as you make your way to Santiago. And don't worry about missing out on the fantastic Galician dairy products, the usual suspects can be found in any market or supermarket in town.

Art and history

Let's face it, the French Camino in Galicia does not exactly have a wealth in monuments or artistic sights. This is not the case on the Portuguese Camino where commerce, trade and demographics led to the construction of outstanding historic monuments unrivalled by any of the other pilgrimage routes in Galicia.

Starting in the medieval town of Tui, with its amazing cathedral, you will make your way to the quaint historic town of Redondela graced with two 19th century wrought iron viaducts that literally cross over the rooftops in town. Pontevedra, with its untouched 18th century historic quarter and iconic churches, would probably be considered the prettiest town in Galicia if it were not for Santiago. Finally, approaching Santiago, you will walk through the quiet Roman founded town of Caldas de Reis with its hot springs, and the venerated towns of Padrón and Iria Flavia, with their monumental churches, monasteries and sites associated with Saint James.

The N-550

Roads are expensive to build, even back in Roman times (a road usually is the cheapest and shortest way from A to B). So it is not surprising that there is a road that lies almost on top of the Camino, which in turn was part of the old Roman road. This is the N-550, and you will be following it from the time you leave Tui all the way to Santiago. Thankfully only a handful of sections are still on this road and in most instances you will not see or even hear it.

The Roman road Vía XIX – the main road until almost the 19th century

The medieval Portuguese Camino followed the existing Roman road *Vía XIX*. This made sense as the old Roman *Vía XIX* would have still been the best road around and it led pilgrims all the way to Santiago. The *Vía XIX* started in Braga (Portugal), made its way across the Miño River at Tui (*Tudela* back in Roman times), went past Pontevedra (*Turoqua*), Caldas de Reis (*Aquis Celenis*) and Iria Flavia. Santiago did not exist at the time so it would have made a right turn somewhere around the Santiago area and continued to the large Roman city of Lugo (*Lucis Augusti*), ending in current Astorga in Castile (*Asturica Augusta*).

Interestingly, if you were to superimpose a modern map with our current major expressways in Galicia (the AP-9 and the A-6) over a map with the old Roman roads (*Vía XIX* and *Vía XX*), these would almost completely coincide.

Napoleon's troops on the Camino

Napoleon's troops would also follow the Portuguese Camino (in reverse) as they attempted to, first invade Portugal, and later at the start of the Independence War, in 1808, subjugate the Spanish insurgents. Several decisive battles during the war took place on the Camino (and the Spaniards won!).

Getting to the Portuguese Camino, getting to Tui

Tui is 118 kilometres from Santiago, right on the border between Spain and Portugal and overlooking the River Miño. Getting to Tui is fairly easy as the town has a train station and a bus station with daily connections to Vigo and/or Santiago de Compostela in Spain. Vigo is the largest and closest city to Tui, and the closest airport.

Although it might feel odd going first to Santiago just to walk back, it may be the only reasonable way for you to get to Tui, especially if you are considering flying to Galicia. Vigo has an airport, which is much smaller and has fewer flights than the Santiago one.

Some pilgrims find it easier to go by bus to Valença do Minho on the other side of the river in Portugal, and start their Camino there.

Here are your best options to get to Tui:

By plane there are daily flights to both Santiago and Vigo from Madrid and Barcelona. For flights and airlines to either airport visit www.aena.es.

By train, your best option is to first get to Vigo or Santiago. Then there's a morning train and an afternoon one from Vigo to Tui, and/or frequent trains throughout the day from Santiago to Vigo. Please note that there is no direct train from Santiago to Tui. For train information visit www.renfe.com.

By bus there are daily services from Santiago to Vigo (www.monobus.es) and from Vigo to Tui (www.autna.com or www.atsahorarios.com). Another possibility is to take the bus from Santiago to Valença do Minho via Vigo, and start there (www.alsa.es). Valença do Minho is literally just across the river and border.

Galicia

Galicia is the northwest region in Spain where the Apostle Santiago's (St. James's) remains are venerated in the cathedral of Santiago de Compostela. The region is bordered by the Atlantic Ocean to the west and to the north, by Portugal to the south and by Castile and Asturias to the east. Galicia, as in Prehistoric times, still remains the most western point in continental Europe (well, *second most*, first is in Portugal). Finisterre is the cape where you can watch the sun die every day at *the end of the world*. Our ancestors must have known this as there was apparently a popular (perhaps even prehistoric) route crossing Spain from Europe to current Finisterre before the pilgrimage route.

Galicia, in contrast to the rest of the Iberian Peninsula (except for the three regions bordering the Bay of Biscay in the north) is green and lush. And that is because it rains a lot more here than in the rest of Spain and Portugal. Indeed, you may have heard the cliché that Galicia is the *Ireland* of Spain. For those that have been walking through other parts of central Portugal, the contrast is startling as you enter Galicia with its forests, grass and rain.

It appears that things have not changed too much since medieval times as Aymeric Picaud described Galicia in the 12th century as being *'well-wooded, with rivers, meadows, and orchards, and the deepest clearest springs, but with few towns, farmsteads or wheat fields'*. I am not sure if I would rely too heavily on the *deepest clearest springs* still being applicable to today; what's more, I normally suggest to the pilgrims I lead to drink only bottled water (you do not want tummy troubles on the Camino) and to not steal fruit from the locals' orchards. However, the rest of the description fits fairly well. Another famed medieval pilgrim, Hieronymus Münzer, also described parts of Galicia as *'good and the little gardens of the city* [Santiago] *are full of orange trees, apple trees, lemon trees, plum trees and other fruit trees.'* Clearly, the availability of fresh fruit in Galicia was noteworthy for both pilgrims.

Aymeric Picaud complains about there being a lack of *'wheat-bread and wine'*. This is clearly not the case nowadays and Galicia is one of the leading producers of wine in Spain, especially white wine. Aymeric Picaud continues describing how there is *'plenty of rye bread and cider, livestock and work-horses, milk and honey and enormous seafish (…). And there is gold and silver, fabrics and furs from the forests and other riches, as well as Saracen treasure'*. Münzer also mentions the availability of fish stating that in Redondela there are *'very abundant sardines'* and in Pontevedra lots of sardine fishing. I must agree again with both pilgrims as Galicia is still famed for its seafood (not only sardines, thank goodness!) and dairy products. As for the Saracen treasure, I am still searching for it.

However, Aymeric Picaud's best description of Galicia comes when he describes the people. He literally says that, *'The Galicians are more like us French people than other Spanish savages, but nevertheless they can be hot-tempered and litigious'* (no offense taken). Unfortunately, Galicians do not fare very well either when it comes to Münzer's description 300 years later, describing the locals as *'so dirty—they have many pigs that they sell very cheaply—and so lazy that they only concern themselves minimally with the cultivation of the land, and live in general from their earnings from the pilgrims.'*

I personally love the last part of the description (*earnings from the pilgrims*), as modern-day pilgrims may (on occasions) be able to relate to similar experiences along the Camino. Furthermore, I am convinced that the same afternoon, in which the remains of Santiago were found, a local set up a stall and started selling mulled wine, and happily started living from his *earnings from the pilgrims*.

Aymeric Picaud and his Codex Calixtinus

The Codex Calixtinus is a 12th manuscript of the Camino de Santiago; or rather, it is a 12th century guidebook to Santiago. It was allegedly written by pope Calixtus II (hence the name) but it's the French monk Aymeric Picaud who takes credit for compiling and editing it, possibly from a range of sources. The Codex is divided into five books, each covering a topic associated with St. James and his veneration. Book 5 (Pilgrim's Guide), is the one that has made the whole Codex famous as it is here that Aymeric describes in almost travel guide fashion the different stages on the French route to Santiago, including suggestions and tips regarding places, peoples and customs.

I am aware that the Codex Calixtinus does not refer to the Portuguese route to Santiago, which had not been consolidated at the time, as most of the Portuguese Camino would have still been under Muslim rule. However, given its historical importance for the Camino, I have decided to include this entry in this guidebook.

The Codex is an entertaining read, even if you are not walking the French Camino, and definitely a recommended one before you start your own Camino. Book 5 can be read for free (and legally) at:

https://codexcalixtinus.es/the-english-version-of-the-book-v-codex-calixtinus/

Scams, annoyances and dangers

The year 2015 will always be remembered as a tragic and sad year for the Camino. In April 2015 American pilgrim Denise was murdered on the Camino. This was the first murder on the Camino in modern history. Denise was walking alone, and she was assaulted on the Camino in Castile, several days before reaching Galicia. Her assailant has been arrested and has confessed. It is unclear what his reason was for committing this atrocity, although the most probable reason appears to have been a *robbery gone wrong*.

However, and although one murder is one too many, considering the numbers of pilgrims, the Camino is still surprisingly safe. And until this year, muggings, assaults or sexual violence on the Camino were extremely rare and usually associated with unwise decisions in towns and cities. Unfortunately, *homo homini lupus*, and in the case of women travelling on their own, or anyone revelling till the wee hours in any of the larger cities, I would exercise the same caution you normally exercise anywhere else. In any case, my opinion is that the Camino continues to be very safe. Since 2015, there has not been a violent crime.

Please note that *you* are safe, but not necessarily your belongings. This means that you may be sharing common rooms with other pilgrims, or be in a crowded bar having a coffee, and all it takes is one bad apple to ruin your day. However, unsurprisingly, the opposite generally happens. On more than one occasion I have had random pilgrims suddenly ask someone in my group if *this was her earring* (she was still wearing the other one and he had picked it up off the trail), or if *this was his hat* (he remembered seeing the chap and his bright red hat at the last pit stop).

Other annoyances are minor, and taking into account the number of pilgrims (and tourists) on the Camino, there are hardly any scams that I am aware of. And people have been scamming pilgrims since day one (the Codex Calixtinus has several examples).

Locals ignoring you

Pilgrims I lead frequently comment on how rude the locals can be, and are unsure if: a) the locals don't understand Spanish, b) they don't understand their pronunciation, or c) are just plain rude. It is usually an easily pronounced buenos días (good morning) that is ignored.

I believe the explanation can be found in the number of pilgrims that walk by the farmer's plot everyday. Assuming that the vast majority of pilgrims do not do the Camino between May and September (which they do), a simple division would give us the number of over 115 pilgrims a day, every day! I would also get tired of saying good morning 115 times a day, every day.

Then there is always the possibility that the local is just having a bad day and feels like ignoring you. Either way, don't take it personally; Galicians are lovely people.

The Camino today

The numbers

As I mentioned previously, after two bleak years, the 2022 Holy Year was extraordinary regarding pilgrim numbers. According to the Pilgrim's Office, in November 2022, more than 438.000 pilgrims had completed their pilgrimage and requested their *Compostela*.

The Camino may be somewhat of a fad that may eventually go out of style, or perhaps the numbers will gradually level out and the Camino will reach its saturation point. What is surprising is that before the pandemic, Spaniards had become a minority on the Camino, accounting for 44% of the total number of pilgrims. A mention must be made of the recent increase in American pilgrims, from just under 2.000 pilgrims in 2006, to over 20.000 in 2019, to currently representing the second largest nationality regarding pilgrim numbers.

In any case, as the Portuguese Camino receives significantly fewer pilgrims than the popular French Camino, even during the peak season it will most likely not feel crowded.

1993

The holy year of 1993 was perhaps the turning point for the Camino as we know it today. Almost everything Camino related on the French Way and that is not a historic monument was put up or set up for that year. This was also the year that the majority of the pilgrim's hostels on the French Way were either opened or refurbished.

Perhaps the next Holy Year in 2021 will have a similar impact on the Portuguese Camino.

The services

The Camino is a big business and once again, it has surprisingly not been developed as much as you would have expected. The large corporations have ignored the Camino so far. Do not expect to see any of the classic chain fast-food restaurants (except in the major cities) or major hotel chains.

The new pilgrim hostels are found mainly within the villages and towns, usually in renovated old homes and injecting much needed funds into these communities. Some are much better than others, and there are innumerable websites on the Internet, which provide up to date reviews of these places. So you might want to consider checking before booking a room or a bed. Bars have also set up rooms with beds on their premises and now call themselves hostels. I would double check before booking. The municipal pilgrim hostels are usually well maintained and charge a *symbolic* fee to cover maintenance expenses (around 10 euros). Many of these hostels are run by volunteers who always have an inspirational story to share. The chapter 'Annex III – Accommodation' in this guidebook offers a list of the major hostels on the Portuguese Camino.

The bars you will see were either already there before the surge in pilgrims or they are new businesses crossing their fingers and hoping to follow the French Camino's success story. In many cases these bars have renovated old village homes and are providing life to the local villages and communities.

For the most part, the Camino is still lacking in sophisticated restaurants and upscale shopping opportunities. And we like it that way! Once you get to Santiago you can indulge to your heart's content if that is your thing.

Small shops, markets and supermarkets, banks and ATMs, pharmacies, post offices and police stations can be found in the larger towns (the ones where you will most likely start a stage).

Coffee in Spain

Here's a crash course in coffee in Spain.

Spaniards mainly drink espresso coffee, that is, coffee that is made with an espresso machine. At home Spaniards tend to use their own espresso machine (George Clooney and his Nespresso are very popular) or an Italian coffee maker. Spaniards steer away from drip. Please note that at a bar or restaurant, the only acceptable coffee is an espresso (funny how this does not apply to hotel breakfasts, even at the five star joints).

These are the types of coffees you can order in Spain and that can be found at any bar on the Camino:

a) *Café con leche (this is your espresso shot with milk, like a latte with an extra shot or a flat white)*
b) *Café solo (this is an espresso shot on its own, your espresso)*
c) *Manchado (this is a small espresso shot with lots of milk, your latte)*
d) *Cortado (this is an espresso shot with a drop of milk, your macchiato)*
e) *Americano (this is an espresso with added hot water, not necessarily drunk with milk)*
f) *Descafeinado (this is a decaf, which can be made with ground decaf espresso style or with a Nescafé sachet)*
g) *Carajillo (this is an espresso with a shot of brandy or aguardiente, only for the very brave (aguardiente is explained on Stage 4).*

Spaniards are not big tea drinkers; they do however seem to have an appeal for infusions such as chamomile and mint teas. Tea will not necessarily come with milk and sometimes it will come with a slice of lemon.

Depending on the time of day your café con leche will come in different sized cups or glasses (without your asking), mornings tend to be larger and sizes get smaller as you work your way to dinner. Spaniards like to finish their meals (lunch and dinner) with a hot drink (coffee or an infusion).

Don't bother asking for types of milk, such as skimmed; Spaniards do only very hot (muy caliente), hot (caliente), warm (templado) and cold (frío). Bars will have sweetener, but not brown sugar.

In 2020, coffee or tea on the Camino cost between one euro and a euro-fifty. Anything above that may indicate that you are being ripped off.

Walking the wilds of Galicia

The good (or bad) news is that there are no wilds in Galicia, at least not where you will be walking. This is not the Inca trail or the Pacific Crest Trail. There is no need to spend all your savings at REI (or similar) to get fitted in state-of-the-art mountain and hiking gear. There are no cliffs to fall off, no walls to scale, no rivers to swim across, no altitude sickness, no water to purify, no animals (not even dogs) to protect yourself from, and even in Winter, there will most likely be no snow or ice.

The wilds in Galicia are rolling hills and farmland, with hamlets or towns every 5 kilometres (or less), some of these with toilets and freshly made espressos (or ice cold beer), and mobile phone coverage 90% of the time, and well-marked and prepared trails and country lanes, and the odd bored sheep or dog that may have a look at you as you walk by. Unfortunately that is all the wild life you will see (except for birds).

The Portuguese Camino is in this respect also a bit different from the better-known French Camino. The Portuguese Camino crosses mainly wine country, walking past vineyards and small vegetable plots. Vineyards represent more tamed landscapes, as pastures for grazing require much less attention and intervention. The Portuguese Camino also runs along the major commercial and communication axis in Galicia that links Santiago with Portugal and Vigo, Galicia's largest city and a major port to the Atlantic. Commerce has led to development, which in turn has led to greater wealth and resources, and this is plainly obvious as you walk the Portuguese Camino. Towns and hamlets have been transformed, with century old homes torn down and newer ones built, urban areas have spread as communications have improved, locals have sought new forms of livelihoods and moved away from more traditional ones... you get the idea.

The Portuguese Camino is beautiful in its own right as it meanders by estuaries and through historic towns, but it's a different beauty from the one you will find on the French Camino. A beauty with many more contrasts.

I must make a final note about the Portuguese Camino in Galicia. This route to Santiago, which at times was more walked and just as documented as the French route (but without the marketing), has over the last decade, enjoyed an unprecedented revival surpassing other routes such as the *Silver Way*. Camino enthusiasts had the historic testimonies and the towns where the Camino passed through were clear, so all they had to do was join the dots. However, just like in the 70s and 80s on the French Camino, pilgrims ran into a serious problem, mainly in the form of highway N-550 as it makes its way northwards to Santiago, literally on top of the historic Portuguese Camino.

Efforts have been (and are being) made to keep pilgrims off the highways and I assume that the aim is to clear all *highway shoulder walking* of pilgrims at some time in the future and provide pilgrims with scenic safe routes. However, this is clearly a work in progress and pilgrims on the Portuguese Camino in Galicia will still walk on highway shoulders (although not many) of all widths. My suggestion is that where the Camino indicates to get off the highway, please do, even if you are sure you will walk a kilometre more. You will not regret the peace, quiet and above all, safety. And if there is no other place to walk but on the road, then please exercise as much caution as possible and walk facing the oncoming traffic.

Finally, the Camino is not a *stroll in the park*; there are times when it can get difficult and if you are not a seasoned hiker, 20 kilometres is a long ways on uneven terrain and in the rain or sun.

Transport

On the Camino you will have three options if you are not walking: taxi, bus or train. There are taxis everywhere (not the actual vehicle but their cards and numbers) and most every bar will be able to call a taxi if required.

By law every Spanish town must have a local bus service, even if it's only once a day or a every other day. This bus may take you only to the next larger town though. All of the main towns mentioned in this book have regular bus services to Vigo, Pontevedra or Santiago.

Even the larger towns do not necessarily have well indicated bus stops. Make sure you ask at a local bar where the bus actually stops (and perhaps for an updated timetable).

If you are considering using the regional train service, the Portuguese Camino sits on two lines. Tui and Porriño are on the Vigo-Oporto line, while the rest of the Camino is on the A Coruña-Santiago-Vigo line. This means that once you get to Redondela you could easily move up and down the Camino via train all the way to Santiago. Remember that train stations are not necessarily near town centres.

Signage and navigating the Camino

Navigating the Camino is easy; just follow the yellow arrows that will lead you northwards across Galicia. And there are yellow arrows everywhere, on signs, on poles, on rocks, on trees... Other signage you will encounter are pilgrim panels indicating the way, sometimes scallop shells engraved in the pavement and random milestone markers (but expressed in kilometres). For the Galicia stage of the Portuguese Camino, there really is no need for detailed maps or GPS backup; it really is that hard to get lost.

Blue arrows?

As you make your way north to Santiago you will see painted blue ones pointing in the *wrong* direction. These blue arrows point the way to the shrine of Our Lady of Fátima in Portugal. So unless you have decided to pay your respects to the Our Lady in the interesting town of Fátima, ignore them and follow the yellow arrows!

What to bring, what to wear, how to prepare for the Camino

Bring a lot less than you think you'll need and leave the fancy gear behind, there's nothing worse than looking like you are on your way to the North Pole as you walk through a farming village.

Some people find that trainers are fine; others prefer their hiking boots (remember that your shoes are your best friend). It may rain and it can be very sunny and even hot. Check the weather and decide. You can always purchase what you need here in Galicia; there are lots of small clothing stores.

Remember that there is usually a bar every five kilometres, so you really do not need that 2 litre heavy-duty water flask. Have a look on *Google Images* and you'll get a fairly good idea of what we look like on the Camino.

And consider walking a little further than the two kilometres to the supermarket and back as your training for the Camino. Age, weight and fitness can be an issue (you are walking 117 kilometres!); however, I have seen all types and shapes reach Santiago with a smile on their faces. It is nonetheless a lot harder than you probably expect, so come prepared, mentally and physically.

You also might want to get your pilgrim's credential before coming; in theory they can be purchased at churches and tourism offices, but don't count on it. You can buy your scallop shell at any of the tourist shops for a couple euros.

The Scallop Shell

It is not clear when or why this symbol came into use by pilgrims. The scallop shell has been used by pilgrims and churches associated with the Camino since the medieval peak in pilgrimages. The Codex Calixtinus in Book 3 refers to the use of Santiago Shells by pilgrims. However, these were seashells that could be used as horns, such as the conch. In words of Aymeric Picaud, the sound from these shells would increase the faith of the pilgrims, protect the pilgrims from the evils of the enemy as well as from hailstorms and thunderstorms. Obviously you cannot use a scallop shell as a horn, but it is interesting to note how pilgrims have always used some type of emblem to distinguish themselves.

There is also a legend referred to as the Miracle of Bouzas, in which Santiago saves a bridegroom from drowning off the coast of Galicia on his wedding day. The boat happened to be the one bringing Santiago from Palestine. The man was flushed ashore (alive) through divine intervention and if anyone had any doubts regarding the miracle, he was covered with scallop shells. Bouzas is now part of the city of Vigo.

Food in Galicia (and Spain)

When we eat

Spaniards roughly eat every 8 hours (7 am, 2 pm and 9 pm), which means late lunches and late dinners for most foreigners. Most restaurants and bar kitchens will close outside of eating hours, which are 1 to 3 pm for lunch and 9 to 11 pm for dinner. These are standard times for restaurants and for Spanish homes. So, if you are planning a dinner out, do not even attempt it before 8 pm as the restaurant will be closed. Or do as the locals, start having drinks and tapas till dinner time!

Spanish breakfasts are referred to as *continental*, that is, a hot drink and a pastry or a piece of toast (and maybe a glass of juice). And this is what you will get at most hotels, hostels and bars. Give up the idea of pancakes, waffles or full English breakfasts on the Camino.

How we eat

The one thing that differentiates Spaniards from the rest of Europe when it comes to eating are *tapas*. Spaniards even have a verb for eating tapas at bars: *tapear*. Eating tapas is a social event and it usually involves drinking several beers or glasses of wine while you share, as a group, small plates of food or bite-sized appetisers. Tapas may be dinner themselves or just a pre-starter course before you make your way to a restaurant for a proper sit-down dinner. Some places in Spain give a free tapa with your drink, others don't. In either case, Spaniards will always eat something while they are having a drink (this rule does not apply to mixed drinks in the evening).

What we eat

You are in Galicia, so your best bet is to eat like the locals. Here's a selection of several classic Galician dishes that you should not have any problems finding (in some cases, it may be the only food available):

a) *Caldo gallego* (Galician soup). Usually made with kale and a classic on any set menu across the Camino.
b) *Tortilla Española* (Spanish omelette). Spain's national dish and found everywhere in Spain. It's really just a simple egg and potato omelette. Particularly delicious in its *bocadillo* (baguette-sandwich) format.
c) *Queso* (cheese). Any of the local Galician cheeses will do you good.
d) *Pimientos de Padrón* (Padron Peppers). These small but delicious green peppers make an unforgettable entrée. Careful, there is always a hot one. See Stage 6 for more information.
e) *Empanada* (savoury baked pastry). Arguably Galicia's signature food. These make great snacks or even lunches on their own. The pastry can come filled with beef, tuna or seafood.
f) *Pulpo* (octopus). A must on the Camino. Remember that Spanish octopus is never chewy.
g) *Lacón* (smoked ham). If you have had enough seafood, this is always a good option. Usually comes garnished with some paprika and olive oil.
h) *Cachelos* (boiled potatoes). Well, the locals are proud of them.

i) *Zamburiñas* (scallops). Not the cheapest seafood you can order but I think it's a lot of fun to be served fresh scallops in their shell. You are a pilgrim after all!
j) *Tarta de Santiago* (Santiago tart). That's the tart with the Santiago Cross in powdered sugar on top that's offered as dessert at every single restaurant across Galicia. It actually makes a pretty good breakfast too!
k) *Mariscada* (seafood banquet). This usually comes as a set menu for two and prices will vary considerably depending on what is included. If you like seafood and want to feast like a king, this is definitely an option where available. Typically, this is what Spaniards will order on a special occasion.

Vegetarians and vegans

Good luck.

Where to eat

Restaurants, bars with restaurants, bars without restaurants, cafeterias... It is hard not to find a place that serves food in Spain. That said, caution with restaurant opening times. Likewise, it's usually wise to have some cash on you as many smaller places may not accept credit cards.

Menú del Día (Menu of the Day)

Most restaurants and bars in Spain offer a Menú del Día for a set price (between 10 and 15 euros). This is always a good deal as it is usually a three-course meal, with bread and drinks (always wine) included. The second course should always have a fish or seafood option as well. On the Camino places are also offering a Menú del Peregrino (Pilgrim's Menu), which is basically a cheaper version of the Menú del día (maybe chicken instead of beef, or one course less)

1200 years of pilgrimages to Santiago.

Since 813 when Pelayo discovered Santiago's remains and Alfonso II ordered the first church to be built, pilgrims have been walking to Santiago de Compostela. Some historians argue that a good part of the initial impulse and continuous patronage by church and state was due to its strategic military and political importance. At the time of its discovery, Charlemagne was busy repelling the Muslim expansion in Europe, and the remains of the previous Christian kingdoms in the north of Spain were doing likewise. To organise a route that would bring thousands of pilgrims from across Europe and through northern Spain would also bring settlers and money to the cities and towns on the route. This would help consolidate the territories that had been conquered by the Christians and hopefully put an end to future Muslim expansion. Giving the Camino religious significance (it is the third most important pilgrimage site in the Catholic world, after only Rome and Jerusalem; and the only one you still walk to!) provided a universally shared responsibility and recognition from the rest of Christian Europe.

By the 11th century the pilgrimage to Santiago had been consolidated and the Camino throughout Europe was patrolled by religious military orders (such as the Knights Templar) and offered a network of hospices for pilgrims. Royalty and aristocracy donated money for these hospices as well as building newer and bigger churches, monasteries and cathedrals. Vanguard artistic and architectural innovations came into Spain through the Camino, bringing first the Romanesque revolution and later the Gothic one from the Cluny and Cistercian orders in France. It is not surprising that that the most important cathedrals in Spain are built on the French Camino, and that one of the first examples of Gothic art can be found in the cathedral at Tui on the Portuguese Camino. The Camino and the steady influx of pilgrims had become a business for everyone and an entry point for new ideas and political intrigues. Monarchs also found time to go to Santiago, such as Queen Elizabeth of Portugal, French king Louis VII or Ferdinand and Isabel of Spain as well as other celebrities such as Saint Francis of Assisi.

The protestant schism, sparked in part by the indulgence controversy (Luther would even question the authenticity of the relics, suggesting that the bones could even belong to a dog!), the expulsion of the last Muslim territories from western Europe in 1492, the on-going wars between European kingdoms, the continuous plagues, and the decrease of state and religious patronage led to a gradual decline in the number of pilgrims.

This decline was exacerbated when the bishop of Santiago cleverly hid the apostle's remains before Sir Francis Drake raided the city in 1589 to the extent that the bones and casket were lost for the next 300 years.

The relics and stone casket were happily found in 1879, during some routine works under the altar of the cathedral, and the pope ratified that they were indeed the remains of Santiago in 1884. However, it was not until the end of the 20th century (and the consolidation of affordable mass tourism) that the pilgrimage to Santiago would return to its former glory, at least regarding the numbers of pilgrims.

And then in 2020 the world (and the Camino) mostly closed down as the Covid-19 pandemic ravaged its way across the globe.

The conspiracy theory: Bishop Priscillian

There is always a conspiracy theory, so here's the Camino's one.

At some time in the 4th century Priscillian was born in what we now call Galicia. He was to become an important figure within the church in the Iberian Peninsula (current Spain and Portugal), becoming bishop of Avila in current Castile. He was also the founder of a heretic religious movement called Priscillianism, which had a significant following in the Iberian Peninsula. Political and religious intrigues led him to getting beheaded in current day Germany accused of practicing magic and fornication.

Now the undocumented part: four years after his death, several of his followers collected his corpse and crossed Europe back to his birthplace. They would have crossed France, the Pyrenees and roughly what we now call the Camino de Santiago. He was finally buried in the region of current Santiago de Compostela. The movement disappeared and was forgotten until 400 years later when a tomb was discovered with the remains of St. James.

The conspiracy theory is that the bones discovered by Pelayo in 813 would be the remains of Priscillian and not of the Apostle James. This is based on the following facts: a) there is no historical evidence that the Apostle James ever came to the Iberian Peninsula, b) the legend that explains the arrival of St. James to Galicia after his death describes how he arrives to the town of Iria Flavia, apparently the birthplace of Priscillian, c) Priscillian was apparently brought back to Galicia and buried in Iria Flavia and d) several anthropomorphic sarcophagi dating from the IV century have been discovered in a church in the Santiago region, which would coincide with the Priscillian events.

The historical accounts

The Italian pilgrim *Giovanni Confalonieri* went to Santiago de Compostela on the Portuguese Camino in the late 16th century, and published his memoirs on his return to Italy. *Hieronymus Münzer* from Germany and *León of Rosmithal* from Bohemia (current Czech Republic) also followed the Portuguese Camino in the 15th century and published books on their return. Extracts from the fascinating accounts of these bygone pilgrims have been included in this guidebook.

Hieronymus Münzer and his travels through Spain and Portugal

In 1494, cartographer and physician Hieronymus Münzer and three friends left their hometown of Nuremberg in current Germany and started an 11.000 kilometre sightseeing trip around Western Europe. A large section of the journey took place in Spain and Portugal.

The detailed accounts of what he saw and experienced has made Münzer an early-Renaissance or late-Medieval tourist and his recollections of the trip were published in his 'Itinerarium siue peregrinatio excellentissimi viri artium ac utriusque medicine doctoris Hieronimi Monetarii de Feltkirchen ciuis Nurembergensis' (how's that for a book title?).

Once in Portugal he decided to complete the pilgrimage to Santiago de Compostela following the Portuguese Camino, the exact one you are on now. He would later follow the French Camino in reverse when he made his way out of Galicia.

Münzer's book is another entertaining read and is now available in English at www.barrerabooks.com; it is a very recommended one before you start your Portuguese Camino.

León of Rosmithal and his travels through Europe

In 1465, nobleman León of Rosmithal left Praga and began a grand tour of Europe that would eventually bring him to Spain and Portugal in 1466. Rosmithal travelled in style and his entourage was made up of at least 40 other people.

Like Münzer, the detailed accounts of what he saw and experienced made Rosmithal an early-Renaissance or late-Medieval tourist and the recollections of the trip were recorded and published by his secretary Shaschek. These were translated and republished in 1879 as 'Travels through Spain of the Baron Leon of Rosmithal of Blatna', by Jorge de Einghen.

As you can imagine this book is not easy to find or purchase and to my knowledge is out of print. It is, however, a fascinating read.

Once in Portugal he also decided to visit Santiago de Compostela following the Portuguese Camino, returning to Portugal by the same route.
Giovanni Battista Confalonieri and his pilgrimage to Santiago

In 1594, the young Italian priest embarked as a secretary on a diplomatic trip to Portugal that would take him from his hometown of Rome to Lisbon. Once in Portugal, Confalonieri would go on pilgrimage to Santiago de Compostela following the Portuguese Camino.

He recorded his experiences in his manuscript, 'Memoria di alcune cose notabili occorse nel viaggio fatto da me Gio. Battista Confalonieri Sacerdote Romano da Roma in Portogallo'. His descriptions and notes of places along the Camino are provided with a more spiritual nature and religious curiosity, and his opinion of the locals and their customs much more honest and detailed.

Camino enthusiasts consider Confalonieri's historical account of the Portuguese Camino as possibly the most rigorous and comprehensive; his account has been translated to English and is also available at www.barrerabooks.com.

The 20th century instigators

It was in France in 1950 with the constitution of the *Societe des Amis du Chemin de Saint Jacques* (Society of the Friends of St. James's Way) when the first major impulse to revitalise the Camino took place. The group, however, was mostly concerned with the historical and academic nature of the Camino as well as translating historical texts.

Spain reacted 15 years later constituting a Spanish association called the *Amigos de Estella* (Estella is a town on the French Camino in the region of Navarra). The Spaniards decided to take the next step, that is, making the pilgrim journey to Santiago possible again (redefining the trails, clearing the paths, reinstating modern pilgrim shelters). The *Amigos de Estella* would publish the first contemporary guidebook in 1969 and the priest Don Elías on the French Camino would publish his revolutionary pocketsize French Camino guidebook in 1971 for pilgrims on foot. Don Elías also sorted out the problem of signage and advocated with local authorities for the promotion of the (French) Camino.

In my opinion there have been five people that should receive a special mention for their contribution to the Camino:

1. King Alfonso II, for his clairvoyance regarding the Camino and because without his royal decree, we wouldn't have the Camino.
2. Brother Aymeric Picaud, for being ahead of his time and writing a *Lonely Planet* guidebook showing us how to walk the Camino.
3. Pope Leo XIII, for doing his job and certifying that the long lost bones were indeed Santiago's, thus reviving the Camino.
4. Don Elías Valiña, for dedicating his life to revitalising the Camino and painting those yellow arrows across Spain.
5. Mr. Ramón Estévez (aka Martin Sheen), for starring in his son's film and thus introducing the Camino to a cohort of future American pilgrims.

Timeline of the Pilgrimage Site

44 - St. James the Greater is martyred in Palestine by beheading.
813 - Pelayo discovers the Tomb of St. James. Asturian King Alfonso II visits the site and construction of the first church is begun.
834 - First church in Santiago consecrated.
844 - Battle of Clavijo. Santiago appears on his horse to win the day for Christian king Ramiro I against the Muslims.
997.- City and cathedral sacked by Muslims.
1075 - Construction of the third and current cathedral is begun.
1122 - First Holy Year declared by Pope Calixtus II.
1139 - The Codex Calixtinus is written by Aymeric Picaud.
1179 - Pope Alexander III ratifies plenary indulgence for pilgrims and ratifies Holy Years.
1188 - Maestro Mateo finishes the Pórtico de la Gloria.
1211 - Current cathedral is consecrated.
1213 - Possible pilgrimage of Saint Francis of Assisi.
1378 - Western schism. Start of the decline in pilgrims.
1488 - Pilgrimage of Ferdinand and Isabel, monarchs of Spain.
1466 – Czech nobleman León de Rosmithal follows the Portuguese Camino to Santiago on his grand tour of Europe.
1494 – German humanist and traveller Hieronymus Münzer follows the Portuguese Camino to Santiago on his tour of Spain and Portugal.
1517 - Start of the Protestant reform. Further decline in pilgrims.
1589 - Remains of Santiago are hidden before Sir Francis Drake's attempt to raid the city. The remains are lost.
1594 – Italian pilgrim Giovanni Batista Confalonieri completes his pilgrimage on the Portuguese Camino.
1879 - Remains of three bodies are found under the altar in the cathedral.
1884 - Leon XIII confirms that the body of Santiago and two of his disciples have been found.
1971 - Don Elías Valiña publishes the first pocketsize guidebook for pilgrims.
1982 - John Paul II becomes the first pope to visit Santiago de Compostela
1993 - More than 100.000 pilgrims receive their Compostela.
2010 - Martin Sheen stars in the film 'The Way', multiplying the interest of North American pilgrims to Santiago.
2020 - The Covid-19 pandemic cripples the Camino.
2023 – More than 430.000 pilgrims receive their Compostela.

Map legend

←←←	The Camino
🐚	Place of interest
🏠	Small town/Village
🏠🏠	Larger town
🏠🏠🏠	Big town
☕	Bar/Cafeteria/Usually food too

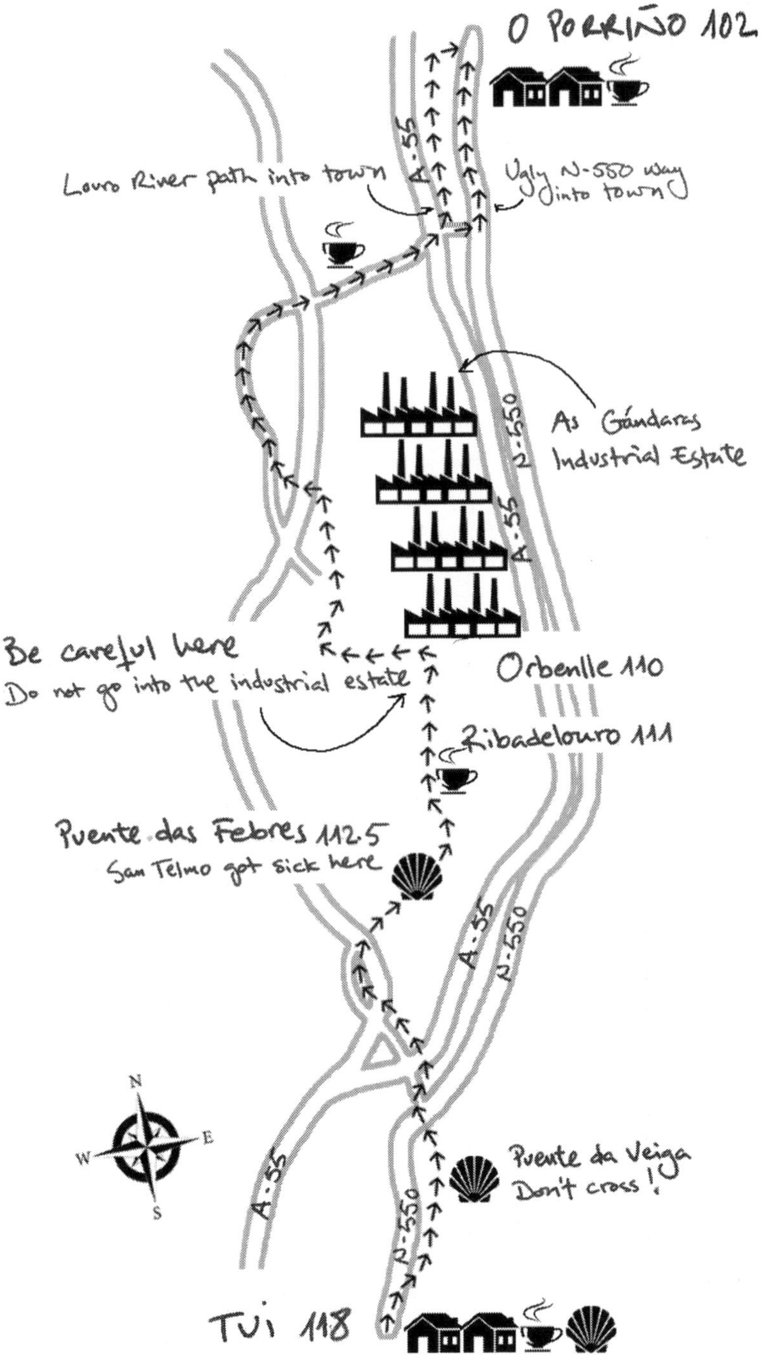
O PORRIÑO 102
Louro River path into town
Ugly N-550 way into town
A-55
N-550
As Gándaras Industrial Estate
Be careful here
Do not go into the industrial estate
Orbenlle 110
Ribadelouro 111
Puente das Febres 112.5
San Telmo got sick here
N
E
W
S
Puente da Veiga
Don't cross!
Tui 118

STAGE 1. Tui to Porriño (+16 km)

Tui is a classic starting point for many pilgrims on the Portuguese Camino as it is the largest town from where you can walk the required 100 kilometres to Santiago de Compostela.

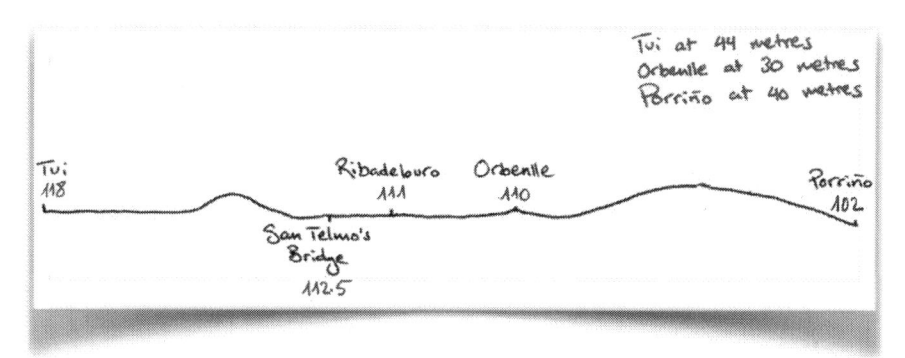

```
Tui at 44 metres
Orbenlle at 30 metres
Porriño at 40 metres

Tui          Ribadelouro   Orbenlle                    Porriño
118              111          110                       102
          San Telmo's
            Bridge
             112.5
```

Nested on the banks of the River Miño and facing Portugal to the south, the medieval town itself and its Portuguese twin across the river deserve at least a day to explore (don't forget that there's an hour difference between Spain and Portugal). This is also perhaps the most challenging stage you will face, as there are a couple of confusing sections. However, the stage is also almost completely flat, and it runs mostly on quiet country lanes or forest trails.

As I mentioned in the Introduction, the Portuguese Camino is a Camino of contrasts, and this stage sums up the following days fairly well. You will have started in one of the most amazing medieval towns in Galicia, contemplated one of the most important artistic treasures in Galicia (the cathedral west door), walked past the first of many Roman bridges as you take your first steps on the historic Roman road *Vía XIX*, admired the serene beauty that can still be found in the wooded areas wedged between motorways and railways, and then in contrast you will also have had a chance to acquire some interesting insight into modern day Galicia and the toll it has taken on the Camino.

Tui (Km 118)

The medieval town of Tui sits perched on a defensive hill overlooking the River Miño. Even if you are not considering going to Valença do Minho in Portugal (see Annex II in this guidebook for more information about Valença do Minho), it is well worth the stroll over the International Bridge across the River Miño as it will give you the best view of the city and a fairly good idea of what pilgrims back in the day saw as they crossed the river (by boat) from Portugal.

The International Bridge

This iconic bridge spanning the River Miño has connected Spain and Portugal since 1885. And contrary to widespread popular belief, it was not designed or built by Gustave Eiffel but by the much less known Spaniard Pelayo Manceboy Agreda, although Eiffel did present his project to the public call for tenders.

This exceptional bridge is right on the Camino and pilgrims cross it as they go over the border. There is a pedestrian walkway and a rail line crossing above. For the best view of Tui, cross the bridge from Portugal on your right hand side.

Although the international border still exists and you do leave a country and enter another, with its corresponding hour change (Portugal is one hour behind Spain), there is no longer an immigration or customs post on either side as both countries have subscribed the Schengen Agreement for free transit of persons within the European Union.

As in the majority of Spanish towns, the old quarter is found in the centre of the modern sprawl. Tui is not an exception, and you will be walking on pavement as you enter and leave the town. However, once you cross the perimeter of the medieval (now gone) city walls, you will feel transported back in time as you make your way through the maze of cobblestoned streets and alleys. And in the heart of the maze is the fortress-like Cathedral of Santa María de Tui, with its stunning west door. Few places on the Camino offer such a spectacular start for a pilgrimage.

Tui is also intrinsically tied to the veneration of San Telmo (Saint Elmo), a Spanish monk born Pedro Telmo who lived in the 13th century. Tradition believes that near here is where the he died on his way to Santiago de Compostela. San Telmo is also the patron saint of Tui, and commonly confused with another San Telmo who lived in the 3rd century, as both are associated with sailors.

The historical accounts

Confalonieri found Tui to be 'small, walled, with few and impoverished inhabitants'. He is however a bit more impressed by the cathedral, which is 'big and inside are the remains of San Telmo, patron of sailors, over whom there is a chapel where he is venerated, although he is not canonised.' Likewise, Münzer also mentioned Tui briefly, saying that it was 'the first town in Galicia, with an episcopal see and a good church.'

The Cathedral of Tui

The fortress-like Cathedral of Tui was started sometime in the late 11th and early 12th centuries, and it was finished in the 13th century. Thus, and in line with many other cathedrals, the style progressively moved from Romanesque to Gothic. Happily for us, there haven't been any major alterations since then and the building has not lost its medieval air. As for its fortress-like appearance, this may have been because at the time of its construction Tui was already an important and wealthy city that was frequently attacked by Saracen pirates from the southern Muslim kingdoms in current Portugal, Vikings from northern Europe or even the not always so friendly Christian Kingdom of Portugal. Don't miss the serene Gothic cloister inside or the views from the tower; they're worth every cent of the euro entrance fee.

However, the cathedral's call to fame is its outstanding west door with its sculptures and decorated tympanum. This entrance is considered the first example of Gothic sculpture in Spain. Playing *Who's who*, and starting from the left of the door and moving to the right we have Moses (holding the tablets with the Ten Commandments), Jeremiah or Isaiah (holding the scroll with his prophecies), Saint Peter (holding the keys to Heaven), Saint John the Baptist (holding the Lamb of God), Daniel (holding another scroll, young and grinning, but no lions), Isaiah or Jeremiah (possibly holding a very liberal representation of the Tree of Jesse, in which case it would be Isaiah), and then a Queen and a King. This royal pair is frequently identified as King Solomon (holding his temple) and the Queen of Sheba (she's conversing with the King and is dressed in a queenly fashion); however, the pair are just as likely to be the less exotic Queen Berenguela (who married Alfonso IX) and King Alfonso IX (who would retake the city of Tui from the Portuguese and grant it royal privileges).

The tympanum describes an unusual Nativity scene with a resting Virgin Mary after having given birth, the Magi in sequence, first speaking to Herod and then presenting their gifts to Baby Jesus who is sitting on his mother's lap, and finally a vision of the Celestial Jerusalem at the top.

Alfonso IX

Alfonso IX was king of León (during his reign, Galicia was part of the kingdom of León) and is credited for not only reconquering most of Spanish Extremadura (western region of Spain bordering with Portugal), but also for having held the Cortes de León, which are considered as the first time in Spanish history that city representatives were summoned by the king and consulted regarding matters of State. He was only 17 when these Cortes were held, so he must have had some really good advisors.

Alfonso IX had a turbulent regency. It kicked off with some serious family disputes about who was the rightful heir to the Leones throne. His stepmother clearly favoured her own son. He was finally proclaimed king of Leon at a very young age, only to find himself wedged between the belligerent king of Castile to the east, the king of Portugal to the west and the Muslim Almohade kingdom in the south. In an attempt to safeguard his kingdom from the Christian kings, he signed a truce with the Almohades, which earned him an excommunication from Rome and a papal blessing to all those who took sides against the Muslims and him. With a mix of politics (marrying first a Portuguese princess and later a Castilian one; only to have both marriages annulled by the pope), intrigue (at some stages of his reign he could count on Muslim troops as allies) and war (battling Castile and later, Muslims and Portuguese) he managed to prevail. Alfonso IX died at the age of 59 while he was on his way to Santiago on pilgrimage. He is buried in the Cathedral of Santiago.

An abbreviated history of Tui

There is evidence of there having been several pre-Roman Celtic settlements here when the Romans arrived in the year 137 BC. The Romans quickly conquered and settled the area, and Tui became an important stop and town on the *Vía XIX*. After the fall of the Roman Empire, Tui or *Tude* as it was known back then, came under, first Suebic in the 6th century (the remains so-called *cyclopean* wall at the top of Mount Aloia on the outskirts of town most likely dates from this time), and then Visigothic rule. Sometime around the year 700, the town appears to have become briefly the capital of the quasi-legendary (and evil) King Witiza, although it is unclear why. Tradition believes that King Witiza played an important role in the events that led up to 711, year of the Muslim invasion of the Iberian Peninsula.

Mount Aloia

Just north of Tui and overlooking the River Miño, Portugal and the Camino as it makes its way north is Mount Aloia. This regional park was the first protected area in Galicia and home to several outstanding historic sites. Unfortunately, it's a long uphill trek to reach the park and to the best of my knowledge there is no public transport, so it is doubtful any pilgrims on their way to Santiago have the opportunity to explore the hill cum mountain.

Apart from the superb views of the surroundings (and they are superb), other highlights are the 18th century Chapel of Julian, the remains of the Celtic settlement of Alto Dos Cubos and the very-hard-to-find remains of a defensive wall that surrounded the mountaintop. This wall (called cyclopean by the locals) is unusual because of its size and length, and that it appears to not be defending anything in particular, as there haven't been any fortifications or settlements found within the perimeter of the wall; very odd if you ask me.

The Muslim conquest and presence in Tui was short felt and the town was quickly re-conquered in the year 739. As the Muslims were pushed southwards with successive Christian military campaigns, Tui would become part of a major Christian repopulation effort that was carried out throughout the Iberian Peninsula. Over time Tui would become a major town on the principal trade route and a military site thanks to its strategic location facing Portugal across the river. Tui has been the capital of one of the seven historic regions of Galicia since the founding of the first Kingdom of Galicia.

Lastly, Tui holds the very honourable title of being the last city to fall to the fascist insurgents during the Spanish Civil War in Galicia.

King Witiza

Witiza lived sometime around the end of the seventh century and the beginning of the eighth century. Historians believe that his death (possibly a violent one and in his twenties) coincided with the beginning of the Moorish invasion of the Iberian Peninsula in 711. Witiza (aka. Witiza the Wicked) is the archetype of the evil ruler, or at least that is what history, tradition and legend lead us to believe. He apparently had an uncontainable sexual appetite and licentious passions, which led him to not only have uncountable lovers and mistresses, but to also murder husbands of women he happened to fancy.

His regency was likewise marked by cruelty, tyranny and sensuality. He is also blamed for having murdered the father of Don Pelayo (No account is given of what happened to Don Pelayo's mother whom he was lusting after), plucking out the eyes of Don Pelayo's uncle, and willingly or (unwillingly) aiding the Moors (possibly not him but his brother, or half-brother, or perhaps his son...) with their invasion of the peninsula.

Toponymy of Tui

The town appears to have received its current name from the Celtic settlement that was here before the Roman conquest of the area. The Romans referred to this fortified settlement as *Castellum Tude*. The supposed remains of *Castellum Tude* can still be visited atop the nearby Mont Aloia (see previous entry on Mount Aloia). Once the local Celtic tribe had been *Romanised*, the Romans would continue to call the settled area by the river *Tude*, which over time evolved to the politically correct *Tui* (in Galician) or the now-frowned-upon Spanish version, *Tuy*.

However, the Romans also felt that the future town required an appropriate mythological founding, or at least the famed geographer Ptolemy did, and decided that a suitable candidate was the Greek hero Diomedes, son of Tydeus, after whom Diomedes would have named the city. The current town has honoured this legend by naming a square in the centre of the town as Plaza Cantón de Diomedes.

It is unclear what Diomedes was doing in southern Galicia after the Trojan War.

The Aloia mares

These legendary animals roamed Mount Aloia near Tui and were believed to be impregnated by the wind. This legend does not appear to be exclusive to Galicia as in Portugal there is a similar myth around the area of Lisbon.

In Tui, but not on the Camino, there is monument to wild horses, which may have been inspired by this local myth, although I have not been able to verify this. The monumental sculpture is made up of three horses running wild; whether or not they are being impregnated is up to you.

Leaving town

I have discovered that most pilgrims tend to find leaving (and entering) towns a much more daunting task than rambling through the countryside. You are much more likely to find a confused and lost pilgrim at a crosswalk or stoplight than in a forest. This makes sense as the signage used throughout the Camino, mainly painted yellow arrows and milestones, magically disappear when in town.

Using the cathedral as the starting point and to leave town properly, you must (facing the cathedral) turn to your left and follow the fairly well indicated route through the historic medieval and Jewish Quarter of Tui that will take you to the bottom of the hill and eventually out of town. The 16th century Church of Santa Clarisa, just before you go through the arched Clarisas passage in the historic quarter, is usually open. However, the Convent of the *Clarisas* cannot be visited, there are nuns inside!

The Camino takes you out of Tui through the backstreets and through quiet residential areas, avoiding the old (but still well used) Tui – Porriño highway N-550, which you will eventually cross. On your way out of town you will pass by the elegant Gothic Church of Santo Domingo (I particularly like the palm trees outside) and the Romanesque Church of San Bartolomeu with its unexpected frescoes inside. Both churches have been altered significantly since their construction in the Middle Ages.

Perhaps the highlight of leaving town is the magnificent once-Roman-turned-medieval bridge *Ponte da Veiga*, which you will walk by but not cross. This is our first reminder that we are indeed following the historic Roman *Vía XIX*. It's also where you will catch your first glimpse of the River Louro, a river you will be roughly following for the next day and a half.

The Camino from Tui to Porriño makes for easy walking, as it is almost completely flat on well-marked trails and country lanes through sections of the A Gándaras de Budiño nature reserve alongside the River Louro. There are however a couple of challenging sections on this stage with confusing signage, and others that take you along the shoulder of local highways or even through industrial estates. Indeed, the end of the stage is the town of Porriño, which is the proud home to Galicia's largest industrial estate and a stark reminder to the modern pilgrim of the cost of development. Although many parts of this stage are very scenic, the stage does, however, present pilgrims with an odd introduction to the Camino, especially if it is your first day walking. In case you are having second thoughts at the end of this stage, please be reassured that this stage is the 'odd one out' and that the rest of the stages to Santiago do not present the challenges that today does.

The N-550 crossing

Caution as you cross this busy road. Then have a look down the road to your right, towards Porriño, and see what you will be missing out on. Most likely the historic Camino travelled by Münzer and colleagues lies under this road as in innumerable cases highways were built literally on top of the historic roads (remember that all Caminos were simply the shortest and safest ways to get from A to B).

Shortly after the N-550 crossing the Camino converges with another local but well-used road, and runs along the shoulder of this road for the next two kilometres (perhaps even a bit more). You will therefore be walking on the shoulder of this road on the right hand side and NOT facing the traffic. Thankfully the designated space for the Camino is wide and you should not feel unsafe at any time.

San Telmo's Bridge (Km 112.5)

About two kilometres from the N-550 crossing you will finally leave the road you have been walking along and enter a small forest. Almost immediately you will reach the picturesque San Telmo's Bridge. The bridge is also called the *The Bridge of Fever* by the locals, as this is where tradition believes that San Telmo fell ill on his way to Santiago with a high fever that would kill him shortly afterwards.

There is a plaque on a stone that reads: 'Traveller, here fell deathly ill San Telmo in April of 1251, ask him to speak to God in your favour.' I am still not sure if this is a kind or an ominous message for us pilgrims. Likewise, I have no idea why the date of his death is incorrect.

San Telmo (Saint Elmo), the saint who is not a saint

Although he is known and venerated as San Telmo, the Dominican monk Pedro Telmo has actually never been canonised by the Catholic Church and remains only 'Blessed' (for the record, that's halfway to sainthood according to the Catholic Church). However, I am not about to debate this with the locals, so San Telmo it stays.

San Telmo was born in Castile towards the end of the 12th century and he died near Tui on his way to Santiago de Compostela. After campaigning with King Ferdinand III of Castile against the last Muslim kingdoms in the south of Spain (he was the king's confessor and confident), he was appointed Prior of the Monastery of Guimarães in Portugal. San Telmo eventually retired to the city of Tui, where he died in 1246 after having started his pilgrimage to Santiago. The Camino goes by the exact location where the saint came down with a fever. Historians believe that it may have been Malaria, a disease that was endemic throughout the region at the time.

San Telmo is well venerated in Tui and throughout the region. He is considered the patron saint of sailors as he is associated mainly with miracles performed or that occurred at sea during storms. With this in mind, it's not hard to understand how sailors and fishermen warmed to his veneration. His remains can be found in the Cathedral of Santa María in Tui.

San Telmo has commonly been mixed up with another San Telmo who lived 900 years before him, and to make matters more confusing, both are *associated with the sea and venerated as patron saints of sailors. However, the other San Telmo was Italian and died a martyr and has been canonised (he is a saint). In a bout of psychopathic creativity, his tormentors slit open his stomach and his intestines were attached to a windlass (a type of pulley).*

And yes, the phenomenon called Saint Elmo's Fire is named after the Italian San Telmo (Saint Elmo).

Ribadelouro (Km 111)

The first village you will encounter after a refreshing walk through the woods is the extravagantly sounding *Ribadelouro* (literally *riverbank of the Louro*), which unfortunately does not live up to its name. This rather dull town is an agglomerate of plain modern homes with a fancy new bar: The *Ponte das Febres* (Bridge of Fever, see above).

The Camino leaves town passing by an intriguing set of five *cruceiros* (stone crosses) in a little park. These mark the spot where the Romanesque Church of Saint Mary Magdalene used to stand. Local tradition believed that Saint Mary Magdelene helped to protect from malaria, which was endemic at one time in the region (this may have been what killed San Telmo). Nowadays, there is no malaria anywhere in Spain.

After another short walk through the woods you will arrive to the first homes in Orbenlle. There's no way you can miss the painted replica of the Portico de la Gloria a local artist has done as you enter town.

Local artist Xai Óscar and his art

Indeed, there is no way you can miss Xai Óscars's tribute to the Camino. The three large paintings are right on the Camino, just above a milestone pointing you to the left as you come out of the woods. In the centre, a painting of the Pórtico de la Gloria (the main entrance into the Cathedral of Santiago); on the right, a smaller painting of a statue of Saint James that can be found on the west façade of the cathedral; and on the left, mirroring the panel on the right, a portrait of an elderly pilgrim.

Regardless of what you think of their execution and style, the paintings do the job of embellishing the Camino and welcoming pilgrims on their journey north. Likewise, I am always astonished as I walk by that the local kids (and/or pilgrims) have not defaced the paintings with graffiti.

To his credit, these paintings were not commissioned, and the only payment he received were headaches with the locals and authorities as he requested permission to hang them in their current location.

Orbenlle and the riverside route to Porriño (Km 110)

Few pilgrims do not recall their Camino through Orbenlle without a smile. Indeed, this unremarkable town has now become a Camino landmark in its own right and the place for many a Camino adventure and mishap.

The main thing to remember when approaching Orbenlle, assuming you want to avoid the industrial estate and walk the riverside (and now *official*) route through the woods, is that you should TURN LEFT at the two milestones AFTER the large paintings (see above *Local artist Xai Óscar and his art*). If you prefer industrial states, than at the two milestones AFTER the large paintings, continue straight on.

As for Orbenlle, this quiet village has been engulfed by the industrial estate to the right and in 2020 all its bars and restaurants had closed.

As you can imagine, the riverside walk is much more enticing than the old Camino through the As Gándaras industrial estate. However, only about a third of this alternative route is actually through forest, vineyards and by the river. The last section is mostly through residential areas and on quiet country lanes, which is still much nicer than the industrial estate.

If you decide not to follow the alternative route through the woods, or couldn't find it and ended up on the route through the industrial estate, then take a deep breath, follow the arrows and do not despair, Porriño is less than two hours away and you ARE on the Camino!

After the woods

The walk through the woods ends abruptly at a large expressway, which you will cross by an underpass. Once on the other side, you will be on pavement and small country lanes all the way to Porriño. You will also be walking through a succession of villages that have grown until melding into each other creating one continuous residential area. Apart from a solitary vending machine (on the Camino) and a small bar (somewhat *off* the Camino to your left), there are no other pilgrim services on this section.

> *As Gándaras Industrial Estate in Porriño*
>
> *Just in case you were wondering, here are some facts:*
>
> *There are actually two industrial estates lining the main expressway that crosses southern Galicia (AP9) and another expressway that runs east-west (A52). Between the two of them they add up around three million square metres of industrial plots and land. They are also part of the Vigo city commercial free zone. The main industrial sectors are textile, transport logistics, automotive related businesses and ornamental granite production from the nearby quarries.*

Porriño (one town, two ways in) (Km 102)

Entering Porriño

Just when you thought this stage could not get more challenging, an alternative route into town is now also being used. So it's decisions, decisions again.

This happens just as you come out from under the A-55 expressway underpass and just before you cross the River Louro. You may see a set of brand new arrows indicating that you should make a hard-left and follow the river (the new alternative route). You will also most likely see, just ahead of you, another set of arrows indicating that you go straight on and ignore the river. I have stated you *may* see the arrows pointing to the new pretty route into town are routinely crossed out and the informative panels that have been put up torn down. Clearly the evidence suggests that the bars that are on the old route into town along the main road are not too happy with the new route.

So the obvious question is which route you should take. Please note that the alternative is roughly the same distance as the classic route.

Here are the pros and cons to both:

The alternative route (assuming you have found it)

This route takes you down along the river and is a pretty walk, mostly in the shade, all the way to the local municipal pilgrims' hostel. A recent local initiative has recovered and made a park out of the Louro River area near town, so do not be surprised to see locals walking their dogs or going for a jog. However, this route is poorly marked, there are very few yellow arrows and unless you have an idea of where you should end up, you may feel lost as innumerable paths trail off the one you are following. There are also several small wooden bridges that cross the river and it is unclear on which side of the river you should be walking. You will also end up by the pilgrims' hostel, which is not in town and on the *wrong* side of the river.

Important: Several yellow arrows have appeared along this river route, taking you away from the river and back into town, most likely past a bar or café. **Ignore these yellow arrows.**

To not get lost, ALWAYS follow the river on the left side, no matter how tempting crossing the river may seem. If you are taken over to the right side then get back over again as soon as possible. And do not leave the river or the trail that runs parallel to it for any reason until you reach the pilgrims' hostel. Once at the hostel, and if you are not staying there, then follow the instructions in the next chapter *Leaving town*.

The classic route

This route takes you along the main drag that enters Porriño. After leaving the alternative route behind you will continue on the sidewalk of the road you have already been following for several kilometres, cross the rail tracks and intersect with highway N-550, which in turn has already become the main road into town.

Once you hit this busy road, turn left and follow it for another kilometre (perhaps a bit more) until you can finally turn off on to a much smaller street (Rúa Manuel Rodríguez) and into town proper. Needless be said that along the N-550 you will walk through the old Porriño industrial estate with all its 1950s and '60s charm. Once in town the Camino meanders a bit, so as to pass by a couple of small churches, and eventually flows into the small pedestrianised historic quarter. This route is well marked and fairly more straightforward than the alternative route. It is also noisy and ugly, unless mid-20th century industrial and urban sprawl is your thing. You do, however, get to visit Porriño city centre, which you may end up bypassing on the alternative route.

I personally would take the alternative route; the walk along the river is surprisingly pretty considering it is wedged between a major expressway, the train tracks and an industrial estate.

Map courtesy of AGACS

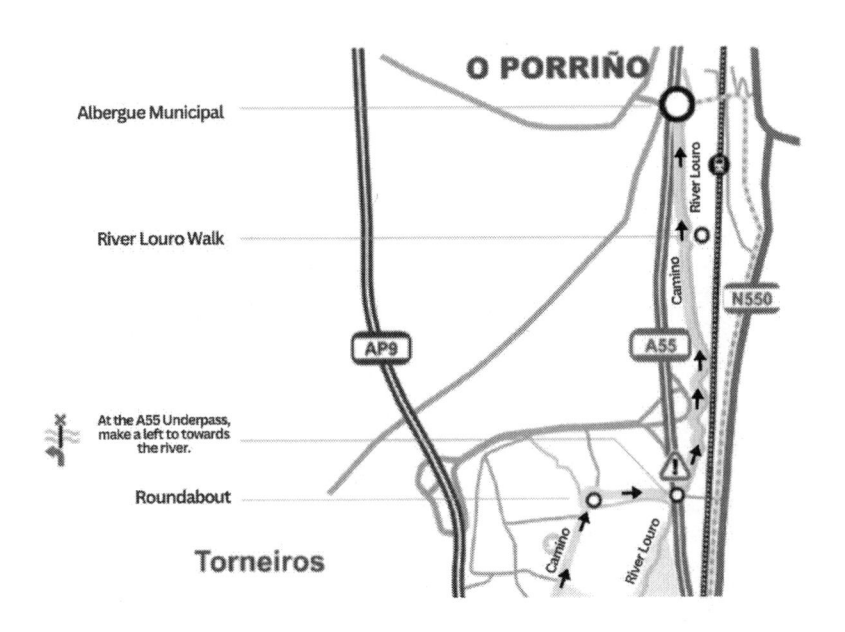

O PORRIÑO

Albergue Municipal

River Louro Walk

At the A55 Underpass, make a left to towards the river.

Roundabout

Torneiros

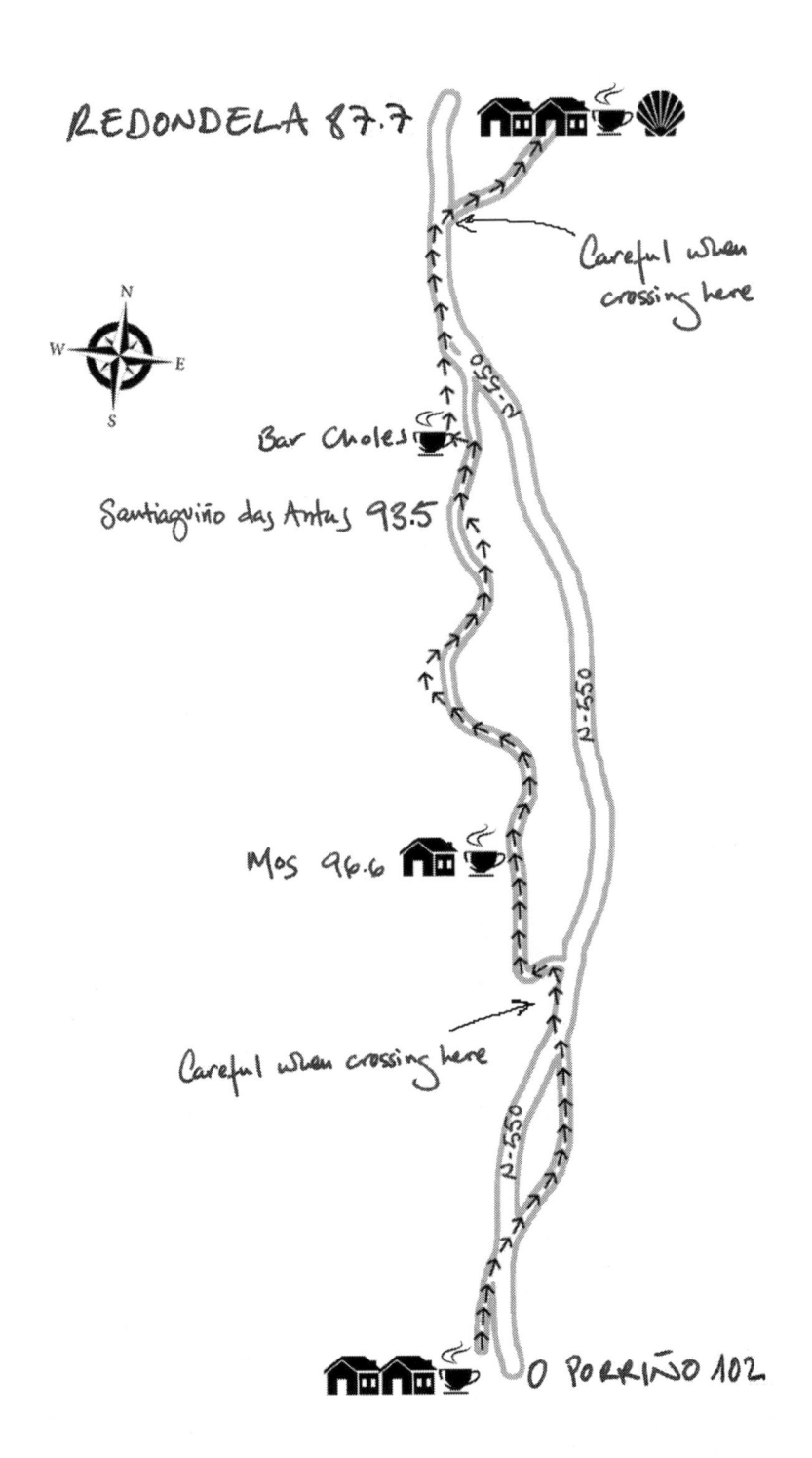

REDONDELA 87.7

Careful when crossing here

N-550

Bar Choles

Santiaguiño das Antas 93.5

N-550

Mos 96.6

Careful when crossing here

N-550

O PORRIÑO 102

STAGE 2. Porriño to Redondela (+14.5 km)

After a (most likely) memorable day walking to Porriño, the Camino takes us straight out of town on small side roads and through the small villages that dot the valley.

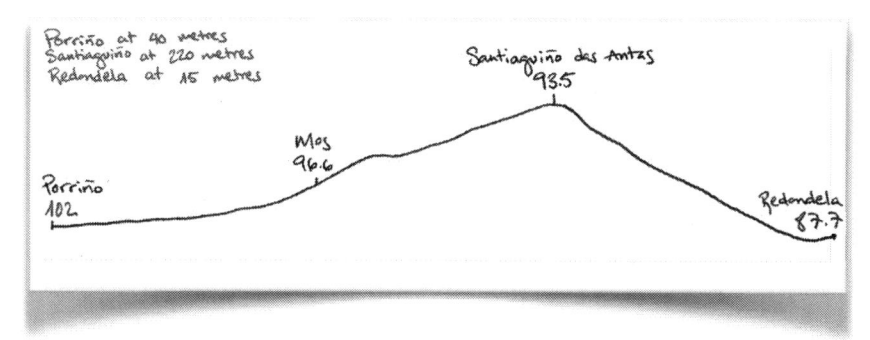

```
Porriño at 40 metres
Santiaguiño at 220 metres
Redondela at 15 metres

                                    Santiaguiño das Antas
                                         93.5
                         Mos
                         96.6
Porriño                                                  Redondela
102                                                        87.7
```

Unexpectedly, the Camino manages to avoid both the industrial sprawl leaving Porriño and the busy highway N-550. The Camino will take you up out of the River Louro valley and over the Chan das Pipas hill before descending into the town of Redondela. Right at the top of the hill just before you begin your descent you will run into a Roman milestone, a reminder that we are still on the *Vía XIX*. Most of this stage runs through the southern section of the Galician regulatory wine classification region of *Las Rías Baixas*, so expect to see lots of vineyards.

O Porriño (Km 102)

O Porriño is, and has been for the last 500 years, an important crossroads in Galicia. The town lies roughly in the place that two major trade routes intersect; one running from Vigo on the coast (Galicia's largest and most industrialised city) eastwards towards Castile, and the other running from Santiago de Compostela towards Portugal in the south. Clearly, this strategic location has also defined its fate, which has transformed a busy small intersection town at the beginning of the 20th century into the location of the largest industrial estate in all of Galicia.

This would all be good news if it weren't for the fact that this has happened on top of a 10-kilomere stretch of the Portuguese Camino. O Porriño is possibly the best example of the contrasts pilgrims find along the Portuguese Camino, where historic routes such as the Camino struggle alongside modernity, and where the cliché of the Camino *being alive* most readily comes to mind as our current needs and values have apparently exceeded our need to preserve our heritage. Apart from trade and services, O Porriño is also known for its wealth in granite that is found and mined (and once, crafted) in the surrounding hills that flank the River Louro valley. Nowadays, granite production continues but has been matched by other commercial activities.

The historical accounts

Unexpectedly, Porriño makes the cut in Confalonieri's account described as 'a small town', and that 'there was a market.' Clearly the Italian was not impressed with the town.

O Porriño preserves a handful of minor monuments, mainly by the local architect Antonio Palacios, as well as a few churches of little interest as they have been restored or rebuilt dotting them with a plainness that most pilgrims find more dull than enticing. Furthermore, if you have come into town following the alternative river path, you will have literally bypassed the centre of the town and its few monuments and sights.

As Gándaras de Budiño

This 700-hectare (1730 acres) natural reserve borders the River Louro north to south as it makes its way to the River Miño. And this is where the Camino associations are doing their best to get us pilgrims to walk, opening new routes away from the cars and through the forests that have managed to survive Galicia's contemporary industrial sprawl.

And indeed you will feel like you are walking in a different place altogether as you leave the asphalt on the Camino and make your way along trails and through lush wooded areas.

Toponymy of O Porriño

O Porriño roughly translates as *the small leek*. Leek in Galician is *porro*, the diminutive being *porriño*. A note of caution for the supermarket: although leek in Galician is *porro*, in Spanish it's *puerro*. *Porro* in Spanish translates as a *joint* (yep, you read right).

So the question is how did this town become the home of the small leek? Particularly as I am yet to see a leek anywhere in Porriño that is not in a supermarket.

Local tradition believes that the town got its name from a Mr. Juan Porro who lived sometime in the Middle Ages, ran a popular inn called *O Porriño* and probably served (little) leeks to passing pilgrims. And as I love unusual explanations, then at least on my part I am happy to believe this one.

There is also another theory (there always is) that traces the name of Porriño back to a local leader who lived in the area before Christ and whose name was *Ghovary the Pueril* (the Young, in Latin). The *pueril* part of the name would have transformed over time to *porriño*. Personally I find this explanation much more boring and as likely as the previous one.

Antonio Palacios

Unknown to many, one of Spain's most notable architects at the beginning of 20th century was Porriño-born Antonio Palacios. In many ways, Palacios was to Madrid what Gaudí was to Barcelona, albeit without the hype and marketing (ok, I am exaggerating a bit, Gaudí was a genius and an artist, and Palacios was just a great architect).

It would be impossible to stroll through downtown Madrid and not walk by a succession of buildings designed by him, many of which are now considered emblematic monuments of the Madrid cityscape. His style can be easily spotted in the monumental Town Hall of Madrid (previous Spanish postal HQ), or the likewise grandiose Cervantes Institute and the 'Fine Arts Circle'. However, Palacios is possibly even better known for having designed the first Metro stations in Madrid, several of which have not changed since his time.

In Porriño there is a monument to Antonio Palacios (a statue of a man sitting on a bench) right in front of the Porriño Town Hall, which was, (yep, you guessed it), also designed by him.

Leaving town

Just when you thought you would be walking alongside highway N-550 the Camino happily turns off to the right and into the anodyne Ameiro

Longo/Chan de Bosque neighbourhood. You will however have had to cross a busy (and dangerous) roundabout and gone under a major underpass alongside the busy N-550 as you make your way out of town before you reach the happy arrow that takes you into the residential area that borders the highway on the right.

Assuming you are leaving town from Porriño's tiny pedestrianised city centre, the Camino will take you to a small roundabout where you will (to the right) walk down Rúa Ramiranes until you reach the first major roundabout/intersection. Leave the large *Gadis* supermarket to your left, cross the roundabout and do not despair as you follow the N-550.

If you happened to spend the night at the Porriño municipal pilgrims' hostel down by the river, or have come in along the river route, then you follow Rúa Peña over the River Louro, across the train tracks until you reach the small roundabout that marks the end of the pedestrianised city centre to your right. Make a left onto Rúa Ramiranes and you'll eventually leave town (see previous paragraph).

Although the stage between Porriño to Redondela includes one of the few significant hills on the Portuguese Camino in Galicia, pilgrims should not have too many difficulties as the country lanes and paths that take you up and over the hill are well paved and prepared and, except for a couple short sections, the ascent and descent gradual.

The first four kilometres out of town are flat until you cross highway N-550 and the Louro River for the last time. Then you will have a progressive uphill hike mainly along small country lanes, roads and streets through residential areas, vegetable plots and lots of vineyards. Needless be said that as usual the signage is spot on, and the chances of getting lost are almost none.

Like most of the Portuguese Camino, once you leave the larger towns there are few services (bars and toilets). I would definitely consider grabbing an espresso in Porriño before you start the day. My favourite is Bar 'X' just as you leave the pedestrianised area in town. The bar is nothing special but you can get an awesome 'X' stamp in your pilgrim credential!

Albariño wine country (and Spanish wine in general)

Today it will be impossible not to notice the dozens of vineyards lining the Camino, many in what appear to be small family plots. You are entering and walking through the wine-producing region of the Rías Baixas. This region comprehends most of the west coast of the Province of Pontevedra, which roughly corresponds to the south-western part of Galicia.

Such as in other wine producing countries in Europe, Spain regulates the wine it produces by certifying the different wine producing regions and allowing the producers to put a Denominación de Origen (designation of origin) certificate label on the bottle (usually on the back at the bottom). If a bottle does not have this certificate, it is probably a mix of excess wine from different regions that may or may not have been aged and has been bottled anywhere. Most of the house wine and wine you will be served with a menu of the day will fall into this category.

So when in doubt at the supermarket about which wine to buy, usually a good place to start is to make sure you are buying a bottle that has this certificate. There are currently over 100 recognised wine producing areas, although most of us only recognise four or five of the main ones (eg. Rioja). Each region specialises and uses its own variety of grapes; however, grape varieties such as tempranillo, are widespread throughout Spain. Here are the most well-known regions,

White wines: Penedés (Catalonia region), Rueda (Northern Castile), Ribeiro and Rías Baixas (Galicia)

Red wines: Rioja (La Rioja region and Southern Basque country), Ribera del Duero (Northern Castile along the Duero river).

Las Rías Baixas is perhaps the most famous of the wine-producing regions in Galicia, and the native white albariño grape its flag bearer. Indeed, many Spaniards actually call this wine by the grape, albariño, instead of using the generic Rías Baixas. But the best part of Albariños on the Camino is that a glass shouldn't cost more than 2 euros, and a decent bottle around 4 euros.

Ameiro Longo/ Chan de Bosque (the N-550 and Camino intersection)

There is nothing worth mentioning in Ameiro Longo/Chan de Bosque except that this is roughly where you will cross the N-550. After walking through this residential area and passing the plaque that commemorates Galicia's most renowned mountaineers, you will eventually run into the busy highway. Follow the arrows and cross to the other side.

You will now cross to the left side of the highway where the Camino gradually meanders up the hill through small villages, country homes, vegetable plots and vineyards, overlooking the Louriña valley. Indeed, until you gain the hill it is improbable that you will walk more than a couple minutes without seeing or sensing civilisation.

Cruceiros

Cruceiros are stone crosses, frequently depicted with a crucifixion, that you will find throughout Galicia. These stone markers served several functions such as to indicate a route (eg. to Santiago) or commemorate a historical event. Most of the cruceiros you will see date back less than 300 years, indeed, there are several modern ones around. However, there have been cruceiros since medieval times.

Veigadaña

This is a typical southern Galician town where it is impossible to know where it begins or ends. However, this unremarkable town hosts a brand new pilgrims' hostel. It also offers some pretty views of the *Louriña* valley below amongst the small vineyard plots. There is also a small monument to a local poet, María Magdalena Domínguez, which I cannot help but find moving every time I walk by.

The poet of Mos

Desde o confín do mundo polo ceo / hai un camiño branco / que guía ó peregrino / desde o confín do mundo ata Santiago

(From the edges of the earth by the sky / there is a white path / that guides the pilgrim / from the edges of the earth to Santiago)

This poem can be read on the sculpture that depicts a woman with an open book on her knees. You will walk by it before you reach the main square in Mos. The monument was erected by the local community in honour of the local poet, María Magadalena Domínguez, who has published several poetry books, the majority in the Galician language. The monument also does a nice job of honouring all the pilgrims on the Portuguese Camino as they make their way to Santiago de Compostela.

In the summer of 2016, María Magdalena Domínguez celebrated her 94th birthday.

Mos (Km 96.6)

Sitting at the base of the hill is the village of Mos (not to be mistaken with *Mos Eisley*; it's doubtful that George Lucas was ever in the region), which unexpectedly boasts a couple of interesting historic monuments and a much needed bar (what a win if the owner had named it the *Mos Eisley Cantina* instead of the duller *Bar O Pazo de Mos*). In reality, there are two bars in the square and another one hidden inside the *Pazo de Mos*. Apart from the bars in the square, which become popular pilgrim hubs at certain times of the day, Mos also boasts the quaint Church of Santa Eulalia (Santa Baia in Galician) that dates from the 16th century, although it has been drastically reconstructed and restored since then. Inside the church, the dizzyingly baroque altarpieces and frescoes are guaranteed to catch you unawares.

However, Mos's call to fame is the 17th century *Pazo de Mos*, which proudly overlooks the small town square facing the church. The *Pazo de Mos* is worth a look inside if it is open; it also has a lovely cafeteria tucked away on the second floor (you can enter from the parking lot to the back). This monumental example of local aristocratic architecture was standing in ruins until 2002 when a group of locals found the means and the funds to restore the *pazo* and provide the district with a space for cultural activities. The *pazo* can be visited in the afternoons. I can only tip my hat to these local community initiatives as since the 19th century the *pazo* has gone from being burnt down by Napoleon's troops on their way to Portugal (it's generally not a good idea to annoy invading armies), to becoming a beef slaughterhouse in the 1970s, to becoming the property of Galicia's leading egg producer in the 1980s, to ruin and nothingness at the turn of the 21st century. The tiny town also boasts a 16th century *cruceiro*.

> Santa Eulalia (Saint Eulalia)
>
> Saint Eulalia lived and died a martyr in 4th century Roman Hispania. There appear to be quite a few Catholic saints who were martyred in Roman times. In the case of Saint Eulalia, her story follows the classic script for martyrdom and then sainthood. At the age of 12 she started expressing her opposition to the Roman gods and challenged the wrong people by expressing her faith in Christ. This did not go down well with the local Roman governor who first tried to scare her into order and then tortured her to death by first whipping her with hook-ended whips and then burning her wounds and hair till it caught fire (imagination and creativity they did not lack). The culmination of her martyrdom happened when she finally died a white dove appeared and flew to heaven.

Santiaguiño das Antas (Km 93.5)

After a placid ascent passing through several villages, you will arrive to the tiny Chapel of Santiaguiño de Antas at the top of the *Chan das Pipas* hill. There are a couple of bars in the area and the usual spread of homes in all directions. Just after the chapel, the Camino takes you by a Roman milestone before it begins its descent.

As you come off the hill you will descend through what appears to be one long continuous residential area all the way to Redondela. You will literally have no idea where one little village begins and the other ends.

Perhaps the most interesting part of the descent is the short section through the woods along a path lined with cyclopean stone picnic tables (I have still not been able to find out what they are) and your first view of Redondela and the Vigo Estuary behind in the distance.

Redondela (Km 87.7)

Entering Redondela

At the end of a possibly strenuous descent from the *Chan das Pipas* hill, you will reach Redondela. Entering town is easy. Once you have passed the last little town at the bottom of the hill and intersected with the N-550, cross the road as soon as possible (before the Camino signs tell you to), so as to avoid getting run over (for some reason the Camino signage has you cross on a blind curve of a busy road), then walk past the Convent of Vilavella (large historic building on your left, which is now an events hall), following the arrows into town on the sidewalk. Be warned that there are two alternative routes through town, which are addressed in the next chapter under the heading *Leaving town*.

The Irmandiños (the fraternity or brotherhood)

One of the most important historical events in Galicia and the reason you do not see many medieval castles was the Irmandiña revolt.

The revolt (or civil war) took place between 1467 and 1469 and it was sparked by the usual mixture of hunger, discontent, abuse and oppression. This uprising can also be considered as the first social and political revolt in Europe, 300 years before the French revolution. The Irmandiños were made up of farmers, traders, low nobility and even some clergy. The enemy was the (corrupt and oppressor) ruling class, that is, the high nobility.

In only two years the Irmandiños destroyed 130 castles and literally checkmated the ruling nobility forcing them to retreat to Castile and Portugal. Unfortunately for the Irmandiños, they were a bit ahead of their times, and the Galician nobility returned with the support of the nobility of Castile and Portugal (and the high clergy), defeated the revolt, detained and executed its leaders (there were, however, no widespread exemplary pogroms or executions and the castles were never allowed to be rebuilt).

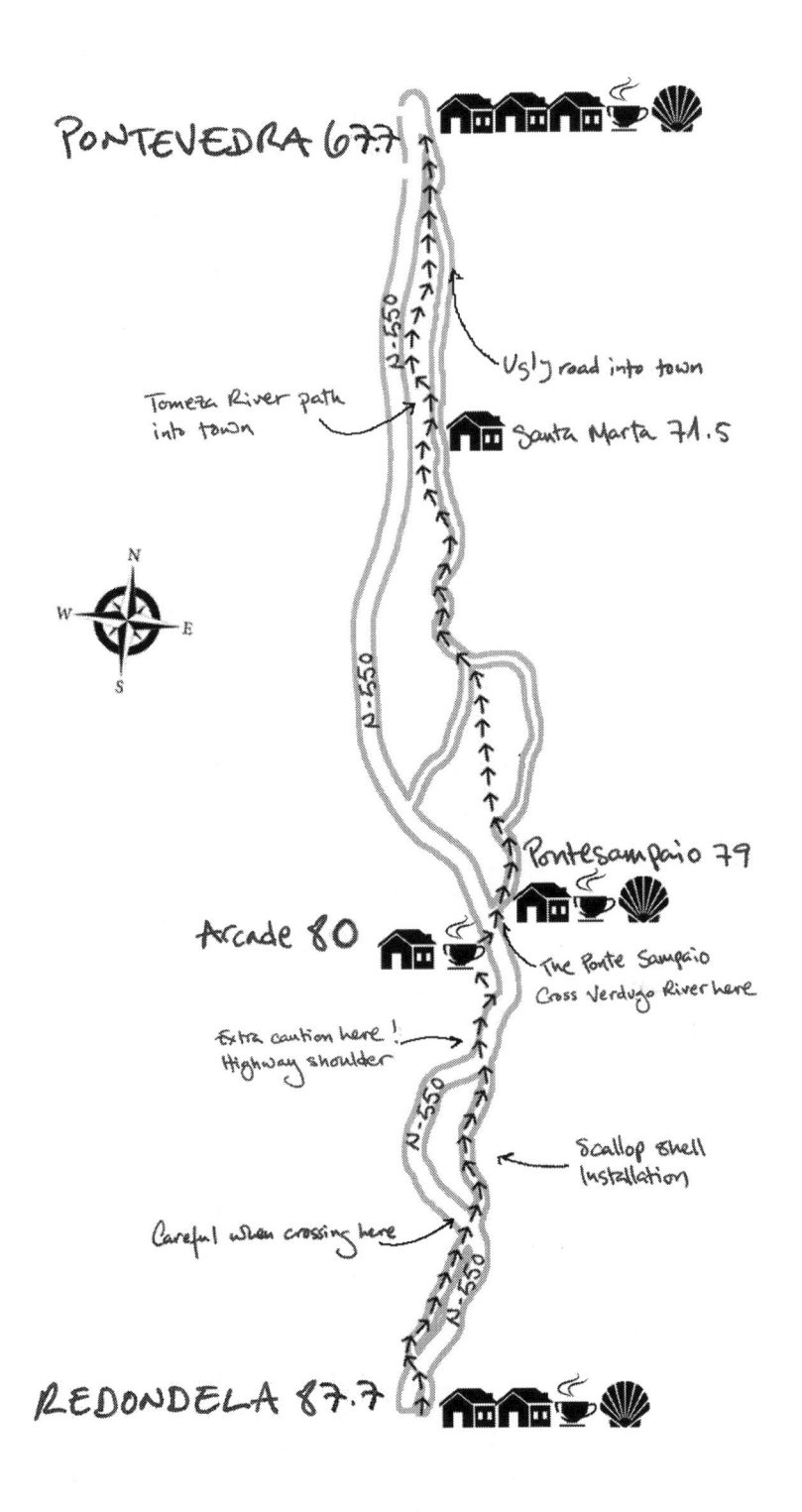

PONTEVEDRA 67.7

Ugly road into town

Tomeza River path into town

Santa Marta 71.5

Pontesampaio 79

Arcade 80

The Ponte Sampaio Cross Verdugo River here

Extra caution here! Highway shoulder

Scallop shell Installation

Careful when crossing here

REDONDELA 87.7

STAGE 3. Redondela to Pontevedra (20 km)

This stage takes you over two hills and offers you several fine views of the estuary that flanks the Galician Atlantic coast.

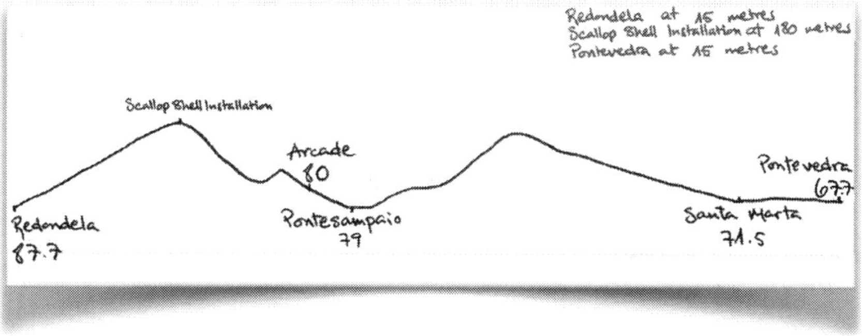
Redondela at 15 metres
Scallop Shell Installation at 180 metres
Pontevedra at 15 metres
Scallop Shell Installation
Arcade
80
Pontevedra
67.7
Redondela
87.7
Pontesampaio
79
Santa Marta
71.5

After coming off the second hill about half way through the stage, the Camino becomes an easy stroll into Pontevedra. This stage also boasts several historic monuments of importance, including the iconic Church of *La Peregrina,* home of the beloved patron saint of the Portuguese Camino.

Please note that this stage also offers an alternative route as you enter Pontevedra. And once again the alternative route follows a river into town.

Redondela (Km 87.7)

Redondela is an amazing example of what an industrial city should look like, but back in the 19th century! And thanks to its vintage industrial atmosphere, the city preserves an unexpected charm highlighted by the remnants of a bygone age of steel and train locomotion. The town is huddled between two hills and the Vigo Estuary and has grown considerably in all directions. As you leave town you will catch a glimpse of the estuary that leads to the Atlantic Ocean reminding you that you are indeed following the coast northwards.

However, Redondela's call to fame is the two historic train bridges or viaducts that cross over the city. Both viaducts date roughly from the beginning of the 20th century and both recall immediately Eiffel and the triumph of steel over stone in modern architecture. Likewise, both bridges are still in use and I have every intention of crossing them by train in the near future.

The historical accounts

Münzer describes the town's location fairly accurately as being along an estuary. However, what really drew his attention was the quantity of sardines that were fished here and the fact that there were no inns and he almost had to sleep in the open. One hundred years later, Confalonieri would describe a large town, 'with 2.000 souls.' He also mentions the estuary and how the town grew along it, and like Münzer, also had lunch here, probably sardines.

But my favourite is the account of the 15th century Czech traveller Rosmithal, who saw to his right, as he left Redondela, the Kingdom of Scotland!

The viaducts

The two rail viaducts that span the town's sky are undoubtedly the most outstanding features of the Redondela. Both viaducts were built at the end of the 19th century, at the height of the 'steel age' and designed for rail transport.

The older viaduct is the Madrid Viaduct; that's the one with the granite pillars that sustain the wrought iron structure. It was inaugurated in 1876. There is a legend that one of the engineers tried to commit suicide by jumping off the bridge when he discovered that he would not be paid as the bridge was apparently faulty. He did not die from the fall and it is unclear whether he eventually got paid. The Pontevedra Viaduct is the other one, made entirely of wrought iron and was inaugurated in 1884.

Both viaducts are currently still in use.

Xan Carallás

The classic 1960s Spanish tourism slogan 'Spain is different' inevitably still comes to mind when you run into the following local legend.

Xan Carallás was, and perhaps still is, Redondela's most famous and beloved citizen. Little is known about him except that he was an uncouth sailor, had bowed legs, was rather overweight and loved to eat and drink (in excess). And that's it, except that he probably lived sometime at the beginning of the 19th century as by the end of the century the good people of Redondela were being called 'children of Xan Carallás'. His popularity *achieved stardom status when in 1967 his effigy appeared on a float in a local parade (eclipsing the rest of the floats) giving out free wine and Spanish doughnuts.*

Local lore has attempted to link him to Redondela's main festivity, the Festival of the 'Coca', which takes place on the day of the Feast of Corpus Christi in June. In this case, Xan Carallás becomes a dragon slayer and founder of the town of Redondela. However, the locals prefer the drunkard and rogue version, and celebrate the unofficial 'Day of Xan Carallás' every year towards the end of May.

Toponymy of Redondela

The name of the town appears to have derived from the Latin word *rotundus* (round), in reference to the *rounded* shape the town has always presented as it hugs the nearby hills and estuary. Although it is unclear if there ever was a Roman town here, there is evidence that Redondela has always been a stop on the Roman *Via XIX* and later Portuguese Camino to Santiago.

Leaving Town

Redondela offers two ways to cross town, both marked and both intersecting at the same place when you leave town. The Praza Ribadivia, just after the tiny pedestrian street, by the bar A Farola is where you must make the decision of which route to follow.

The classic one takes you from the *Praza Ribadivia* into the old quarter of town, past the Town Hall, up and down narrow residential streets, some cobblestoned, until intersecting with the N-550 as it leaves town. Apart from it being quiet and serene, there really is not much else happening on this route.

The newer route is the one I find much more interesting as it allows for different views of the viaducts that hover over the city and goes by many more bars (also a necessity before you start walking). This route is marked with fancy new Camino signs that include an Internet service advertisement. It branches off from *Praza Ribadivia* down the tiny pedestrianised *Rúa Casta San Pedro* where it then intersects with the large boulevard *Paseo Xunqueira*. Turning right, there is no way to get lost as you follow the boulevard that runs parallel to the river until you intersect with the N-550, which will appear from a bridge behind you. Stay on this main road until the Camino turns off to your left as you leave town. You should not leave town on the N-550!

> *La Coca*
>
> *The Coca was a dragon that lived in the waters near Redondela and terrorised (and devoured) the locals, with a special preference for the prettiest maidens (it's always the prettiest maidens). The dragon was killed by a valiant young sailor who, hearing the maidens' cries as he was sailing by, rallied the local young men and together they killed the dragon. This happened in the 15th century on the day of Corpus Christi.*
>
> *In commemoration of this event, the yearly Feast of Corpus Christi procession is led by a dragon (la Coca), followed by dancing young men with swords, and dancing women that are carrying little girls on their shoulders. I have always found it intriguing how obvious pagan elements have been completely integrated into major Feasts in the Catholic calendar, in this case, the Feast of Corpus Christi, which celebrates the very solemn miracle of the transubstantiation of the bread and wine before the Eucharist.*

Exercise caution as you cross the intersection and N-550 after leaving the residential area of Redondela, which has become the hamlet of Cesantes without your realising it. Cars and trucks literally fly down the hill and around the bend. After crossing the highway, you still have a bit more pavement walking till you finally make your way into the wooded areas and paths up on the hill. It is up on the Lomba hill between Redondela and Arcade when you will finally get a fantastic view of the Vigo Estuary. These are the sections and moments that make the Portuguese Camino unique from the other inland Camino routes that cross Galicia.

The Scallop Shell Installation

Right at the top of the hill and before you start your descent into Arcade, you will pass by the Scallop Shell Installation. This intriguing display of framed scallop shells, most of them decorated with notes and messages is a pleasant surprise. I am still investigating who set it up and what was the reason (if any). Particularly moving are a couple shells that remember the death of pilgrim Denise (see the Introduction chapter for more information regarding pilgrim Denise).

San Simón Island

The picture perfect San Simón Island is connected to the smaller San Antón by a bridge. Both lie in the Vigo Estuary, just off the coast facing the town of Cesantes and both are only accessible by boat.

The first account we have of the island was in 997, when refugees from an invading Muslim army were slaughtered on the island. Once the Arabs were expelled from Galicia, the religious-military order of the Knights Templar set up a base on the island and built the Church of Saint Simon (long gone). After the forced dissolution of the military order in the 14th century, the island became property of the Crown of Castile. One hundred years later, at the beginning of the 16th century, the Franciscans set up base here and founded a monastery, which they were forced to abandon by the end of the same century following continuous attacks by pirates, amongst them Francis Drake. The Benedictines, ever alert, found their way to the island and decided to use the former Franciscan monastery at the turn of the 17th century. However, their stay here was short as the Franciscans quickly returned and exercised their rights over the island and the monastery. In the 18th century the Franciscans were forced to escape the island again, this time permanently, due to the hostilities between the English-Dutch armies and the Spanish-French ones at the Battle of Rande.

In the 19th century the islands became a leper colony. San Simón operated as a quarantine post while lepers without cure were confined on the smaller island of San Antón (at the time there was no bridge). In the 20th century and during the Spanish Civil War, the island became a notorious concentration camp and later a prison, which was run by the Fascist insurgent army. It would continue to serve the repressive regime as a prison for political prisoners until after the Civil war, when it was finally closed in 1943 and abandoned.

The island was reopened in 1999 and has become a popular tourist attraction in the area. Locals are also proud of the island for being the supposed birthplace of the medieval troubadour, Meendiño, who recalls the island in his verses:

*Sedia-m' eu na ermida de San Simión
e cercaron-mi-as ondas que grandes son.
Eu atendend´o meu amigu'*

*I was sitting at the shrine of San Simeon
And the waves surrounded me, how high they were,
Me waiting for my friend.*

> **Battle of Rande**
>
> At the start of the War of the Spanish Succession an important naval battle was fought in the Vigo estuary between English and Dutch forces (members of the Grand Alliance), and Spanish and French ones (House of Bourbon). This battle is known as the Battle of Rande.
>
> Although the battle is considered part of the War of the Spanish Secession, the truth is that the military engagement was motivated by an act of piracy or pillage against Spanish vessels. These had just arrived, escorted by the French navy, from the Americas with an important cargo of silver. British intelligence had found out about the value of the cargo and had redirected the Anglo-Dutch fleet to Vigo where the Franco-Spanish fleet was due to arrive. In this manner, both fleets engaged in the estuary of Vigo, just off the Redondela coast. A painful defeat was inflicted on the Franco-Spanish fleet, which was completely destroyed or captured. However, apart from a boost in their pride and several ships, the Anglo-Dutch fleet left Vigo empty handed. The treasure was either unloaded before the battle, or sunk to the bottom of the estuary.
>
> Jules Verne in his novel Twenty Thousand Leagues Under the Sea uses this legend to explain Captain Nemo's vast fortune. There is a monument of two divers and Captain Nemo just off the nearby island of San Simon commemorating this literary reference. Unfortunately it is fairly off the Camino and hard to access unless the tide is very low.

As you come off the hill you will intersect again with the N-550 and you will have to walk about half a kilometre on the very narrow shoulder the road provides. Please walk facing the traffic.

Arcade (Km 80)

This modern overgrown summer resort town has spread along the N-550 and most of the estuary coastline. Arcade receives a fair share of pilgrims during the year, but its main visitors are the local summer revellers that flock from the nearby cities looking for beaches and seaside fun. The town is also home to the yearly *'Fiesta de la Ostra'* (Oyster Festival) that takes place in spring. And indeed oysters are a local specialty here as the estuary waters are apparently *just perfect* for their farming.

Arcade is a very convenient, albeit unremarkable, pit stop after Redondela and offers an array of bars and cafeterias along the Camino as it makes its way through town. Please note that you will cross and leave Arcade through the backstreets and not on the main street/road/N-550. In other words, as you leave town, if you are crossing the Verdugo River on a modern steel bridge and not on a historic stone bridge, you are NOT on or even close to the Camino!

Castle of Soutomaior and Pedro Madruga

At the top of the Viso Hill and several kilometres from Arcade sits the 12th century Castle of Soutomaior. Unfortunately it is too far off the Camino to walk to. Soutomaior is one of the best-preserved castles in Galicia and, although it was partially destroyed during the Irmandiño revolt of the 15th century (see Irmandiño entry in Stage 2), it was rebuilt in that same century by Pedro Álvarez e Sotomaior, better known as Pedro Madruga.

Pedro Madruga purportedly got the nickname 'Madruga' (early riser) because of his annoying habit of going in to battle at dawn, something apparently unusual at the time amongst his peers. Pedro Madruga was a prominent figure in late medieval Galician history and head of the most important family in southern Galicia at the time. During the Irmandiño revolt, Pedro Madruga led the offensive against the peasants rallying the Galician nobility against the Irmandiños and with the support of the King of Portugal. He would also become actively involved in the Castilian War of Succession in the late 15th century. Unfortunately for him he supported the side that lost, which meant a steady and gradual decline in his power and influence until his death in 1486.

There's a fantastic farfetched theory that suggests that Christopher Columbus was in reality Pedro Madruga. Apparently, amongst other reasons, there is a 16th century text claiming that Diego de Soutomaior was Colombus's son, and we know that Pedro Madruga had a son by the same name. Colombus, apparently, also displayed Portuguese mannerisms, which would have been very similar to Galician ones, and not the expected Italian ones.

Pontesampaio (Km 79)

The small proud town of Pontesampaio is everything Arcade isn't. The town has a brilliant historical record, is accessed by a medieval bridge that gracefully spans the River Verdugo and its tiny narrow alleys are lined with smaller homes that have conserved the labyrinth-like layout of the town. Elderly locals stay fit as they climb up and down the steep slopes to and from their homes. Be warned that as you come over the bridge, signage is sparse and hard to spot.

Battle of Pontesampaio

If one famous battle was not enough, this section of the Camino is also the site of the most celebrated battle in Galicia during the Spanish War of Independence in 1809. Napoleon had not only outstayed his welcome in Spain, but had decided to alter his agreement with the Spanish monarchy, occupy Spain and place his brother on the Spanish throne. Spain has clearly had its share of inept rulers throughout history.

At the bridge of Pontesampaio, which you will cross as it is on the Camino, an irregular force of Spanish soldiers and armed locals stopped and defeated the 10.000-strong French army that was marching towards the strategic city of Vigo. Less than a month later, the last French soldier had retreated from Galician soil.

The locals are rightly proud of the feat and there are several commemorative plaques and panels on either side of the bridge.

After leaving Pontesampaio you will make your way up and over the Cacheiro hill, which will bring you into the Tomeza valley. Once again the Camino is a mix of country lanes and manageable dirt trails, another small Roman bridge and the remains of the ancient Roman road!

Tomeza Valley and Bertola district

As you come off the hill and make your way down to Bertola and the River Tomeza, you will walk by the inconspicuous *Fonte Figuerido* and its picnic area. The locals nonetheless are furiously proud of the water from the fountain, which apparently comes from a spring just up the hill, and it is not unusual to see them filling jugs and bottles to take back home. Why exactly they prefer this water to the local tap water is a mystery. And after chatting with a local for almost an hour I was still left in the dark.

Just after the fountain and after having crossed the small road that links all the towns in the Tomeza Valley, you will walk by a small (seasonal) bar, undoubtedly geared for pilgrims and their needs.

Santa Marta and the alternative river route into town (Km 71.5)

After a pleasant three-kilometre stroll, you will enter the village of Santa Marta. As usual, it is almost impossible to figure out where these towns begin and end. Santa Marta has a lovely little Romanesque-looking restored church, which is usually open and has a stamp. There is also a *cruceiro* by the church. As you leave town you will converge with the main road that leads into Pontevedra (not the N-550). Where this happens you will also encounter a signpost offering an alternative route into Pontevedra following the River Tomeza.

So again the question that arises is which route you should take. Please note that in this case, the alternative is significantly longer (possibly up to two kilometres) than the classic route.

Here are the pros and cons to both:

The alternative river route

This route takes you to the left down to the river, and it is an absolutely stunning stroll through the woods, along the river and on a dirt trail, away from the road and motor traffic. Finding this trail requires a small leap of faith. Once you make the left at the River Tomeza signpost, follow the small road for roughly 500 metres until you reach a curve. At this curve you will see a dirt trail branching off to the left (the small road continues; ignore it), there should be arrows leading down here. Follow this dirt trail until you reach a small bridge that crosses the river. Once you cross the bridge make a hard RIGHT and follow the river into town. Do not expect to see many arrows again until you are in Pontevedra. If in doubt, always stay by the path that follows the river. Likewise, what the locals call a river is more like a stream, and that the trail becomes a tiny narrow path in some sections as it hugs the riverbank.

The trail ends in Pontevedra town just before the train station and just after a large stone underpass that you will walk under; you will have walked under another large underpass (not stone) previous to this one.

Warning: The ongoing 'arrow war' on this route, with local bars painting arrows taking you off the river route and to their bars on the road, which are on the old-classic route into Pontevedra. You probably do not want to do this, as you will end up walking into town along the boring and dangerous road. So, ignore the arrows, have faith and follow/hug the river trail until literally you are ejected from it as there will be nowhere else to go.

The classic route

This route keeps you on the main road into town and is shorter than the alternative one as it follows a straighter line. There is absolutely no way you can get lost as you follow the road and there are also plenty of arrows. The drawbacks are obvious.

Once again, I personally would take the alternative route, as the walk along the river is magical; and if you follow the river, it is hard to get lost.

Santa Marta

Santa Marta is the patron saint of housewives, cooks, servants and the home in general. She is also the saint you pray to if you have an unfaithful or difficult husband. With these attributes, it's not surprising that she is one of the most popular and venerated saints in the Catholic world.

In the Gospels, Marta is contemporary to Jesus, received him in her home and may have been at the crucifixion. She was also Lazarus's sister. Later medieval legends add that she was also sister to Mary Magdalene, whom she accompanied to southern France after the death of Jesus. In France, amongst other miracles, she helped defeat a dragon and resurrected a drowned man.

Santa Marta is usually represented with an aspersorium and aspergillum (small bucket and a sprinkler for holy water).

Pontevedra (Km 67.7)

Entering Pontevedra

Unsurprisingly, the two-kilometre walk into and across modern Pontevedra is far from fetching. However, within the city, the Camino is well marked with yellow arrows making the streets and intersections easy enough to navigate. The main highlights you will see as you walk towards the city centre are the train and bus stations, surrounded by the usual assortment of fast food restaurants.

I have considered the centre of the city, and therefore the end of this stage, the Church of *La Peregrina* (The Lady Pilgrim) with its iconic scallop-shaped floor plan. *La Peregrina* is right on the edge of the almost-pedestrianised historic quarter.

CALDAS DE REIS 44

Cross Umia River to enter town

Tivo 46.8

2-550

Extra caution here! Highway shoulder

Río Barroso Waterfalls 1 km from The Camino

51

Bar A Eira

2-550

San Amaro 57.5

PONTEVEDRA 67.7

2-550

Cross Lérez River to leave town

STAGE 4. Pontevedra to Caldas de Reis (23.7 km)

This is one of the longest stages you will walk on your way to Santiago de Compostela. However, as it is almost completely flat, most pilgrims do not find it too challenging.

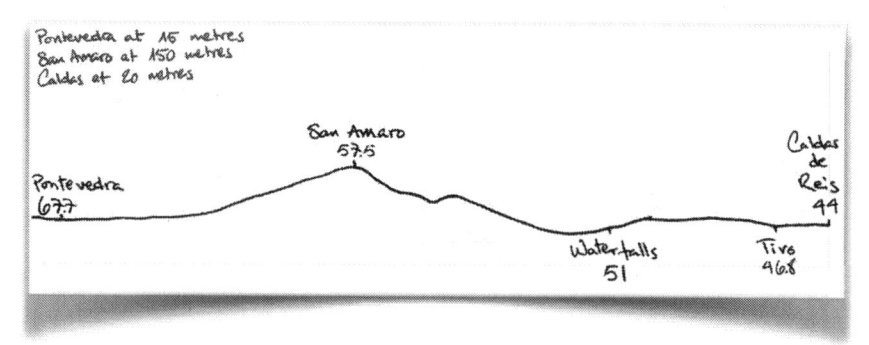

```
Pontevedra at 15 metres
San Amaro at 150 metres
Caldas at 20 metres
```

Elevation profile: Pontevedra 67.7 – San Amaro 57.5 – Waterfalls 51 – Tivo 46.8 – Caldas de Reis 44

As in previous days, the Camino runs parallel along small country lanes and trails to the N-550 but not near enough to be bothered by it or its traffic. This whole stage goes through the northern section of the Galician wine region of *Las Rías Baixas*, so like on Stage 2, expect to see lots of vineyards again!

Pontevedra (Km 67.7)

The small city of Pontevedra stands out on the Portuguese Camino as an appetiser to what you will see and experience in Santiago. Indeed, the whole city appears as a miniature scale of Santiago. On the other hand, the modern part of the city provides for any service pilgrims may require. There's even a Burger King in the historic quarter if you feel you need some comfort food (sorry, the McDonald's is not in town). So, if you are considering taking a day off on your Camino, and you are not looking for isolation, then Pontevedra is probably your safest bet as it has an ample range of accommodation, restaurants and sights to keep you entertained for at least a full day.

The historical accounts

In the 15th century Münzer briefly described Pontevedra as a 'very old city and not very big, but with a good seaport and with a lot of sardine fishing, the main food in that region. There is also a river and a solid bridge with fourteen arches.' It appears that Münzer was not very good at counting as

> the bridge only has eleven arches. Likewise, in the 16th century, Canfalonieri counted 13 arches, which is closer to fourteen than eleven, making us wonder if the bridge has not lost a couple arches since the 16th century. Confaolinieri also described the city as being well fortified with a wall and with a port with many ships, describing how 'boats arrive here with the tide from Sevilla'. Clearly the size and activity of the port impressed both pilgrims. As for the town itself, Confalonieri is less enthusiastic: 'The Church of Saint Francis is big and it is poorly roofed. The town has another two, which are good. The houses, as usual, small, almost all of them with wooden roofs that overhang on narrow alleys.' One of the other two churches he refers to may have been the Church of San Domingo, as it would have definitely stood out because of its size and importance. It is currently in ruins and part of the Museum of Pontevedra.
>
> Neither Münzer nor Confalonieri would have seen La Peregrina as it was built at a later date.

Toponymy of Pontevedra

There appears to be a unanimous consensus that the name of the town comes from the Latin words *pons* and *veter*, the first meaning *bridge* and the second *old*. These two words evolved over time becoming in the Middle Ages *Ponte Vetera* and finally into *Pontevedra* as we know it today.

There has been a bridge spanning the River Lérez (and therefore part of the *Vía XIX* and the Camino de Santiago) since anyone can remember and before you, literally hundreds of thousands of pilgrims have crossed this same bridge. I personally love this idea.

Abbreviated history of Pontevedra

Tradition believes that the city was founded by the Greek hero Teucrus, and the Town Hall backs this claim with the following text on its façade: FVNDOTE TEVCRO VALIENTE/DE AQVESTE RIO EN LA ORILLA/PARA QUE EN ESPAÑA FVESES/DE VILLAS LA MARAVILLA (or in English: Courageous Teucrus founded you/by the banks of this river/so that in Spain you would be/a marvel amongst cities).

> *Teucrus*
>
> *Greek prince, famed archer and half-brother to superhero Ajax, Teucrus distinguished himself at battle at Troy and then later by conquering the island of Cyprus. Apparently he also travelled to Galicia.*

However, most likely its origin was much less exciting. There appears to be evidence that on the spot where the Roman Bridge (Now the Burgo Bridge) crossed the River Lérez on the *Vía XIX*, there was a small Roman settlement, or perhaps just a large Roman villa. Given its strategic location, this settlement would have gradually grown into a proper town.

Pontevedra would continue to grow throughout the Middle Ages becoming Galicia's most populated city and a main ocean port in the 16th century. Pontevedra would even rival other European ports in sea trade during the late Middle Ages, which may be surprising for current pilgrims to believe as the city no longer represents a busy port nor does it appear to have access to the Atlantic Ocean. Indeed, Pontevedra's shipyards were large enough to have built Christopher Columbus's largest ship, the Santa María.

The decline in trade, mainly with Portugal, and the rise of other ports on the Galician coast (e.g. Vigo), led to a gradual decline in the city's fortune during the following centuries. This decline has been somewhat reversed in the last century with its designation as administrative capital of the province and the growth in tourism. Unfortunately for Pontevedra, it is just too close and resembles too much Santiago de Compostela, so mainstream tourist routes often skip it.

La Peregrina

No matter how pretty the town is, Pontevedra's call to fame is its church *La Peregrina*.

This 18th century church houses the image of the patron saint of Pontevedra and of the Portuguese Camino, the Virgin Mary Pilgrim, known as *La Peregrina* (The Lady Pilgrim). It is not clear when or why the veneration of our Lady the Pilgrim started.

The church, in the shape of a scallop shell (the floor plan) was paid for by the local religious association with the very long name of the *Cofradía de Nuestra Señora del Refugio y Divina Peregrina*.

Mounted on the façade of the church and facing the pilgrims as they approach are the statues of *La Peregrina,* with Sant Roch and Santiago on either side of her. Above the three of them and crowning the façade is an image of Christ. The fountain in front of the church between the two sets of stairs has an unusual sculpture of a man holding the jaws of a lion. This image could be associated with Daniel in the Old Testament, or even Hercules during one of his tasks. However, the figure is supposed to depict Teucrus, legendary founder of the city of Pontevedra. Apparently, when the local artist received the commission, he had no idea who Teucrus was, so he decided to represent another Greek mythological character: Hercules and the Nemean lion.

Other sights around town

Church of San Francisco

Just around the corner from *La Peregrina* stands the Church of San Francisco, dating back to the 13th century. The building next to it, currently the local Tax Revenue Office, used to be part of the Franciscan convent.

Basilica of Santa María

The rather sombre and bulky Basilica of Santa María stands out in Pontevedra thanks to its size and its commanding location overlooking the river and most of town. However, the church may not completely meet your aesthetic expectations due to the lack of harmony and balance between the different styles that make up the building, with late Gothic styles (15th century) clashing with elements of Spanish Renaissance (16th century).

The Basilica is not on the Camino and visiting it requires a short (and very pretty) detour through the oldest section of the historic quarter.

Convent de Santa Clara

Dating back to the 13th century, the convent sadly closed its doors in September 2017 when the last three nuns were transferred to another convent. Even sadder is that the local brides-to-be no longer have a place to take eggs so as to ensure good weather on the day of their wedding.

The convent and church can be found on the Rúa Santa Clara, which is a 10-minute stroll from the Camino as it makes its way through the pedestrianised part of town.

Santa Clara's eggs

Traditionally, future brides took and gave a dozen eggs to their local Clarisa convent to ensure good weather at her wedding. This tradition/ritual is surprising still fairly common in current Spain.

But why Santa Clara? It appears that Santa Clara (Saint Clare) was chosen as in Spanish an 'egg white' is a 'clara de huevo' and a 'clear day' is a 'día claro'; Makes sense.

Little John or Sister María?

Perhaps the most unusual story associated with the Convent of the Clarisas is the story of Sor María de San Antonio (Sister Mary of San Antonio), who was also known as Little John (Juanico).

Apparently, back in the 16th century, a wealthy and becoming teenager from Toledo fled her home, escaping from her father and her suitors. Determined to dedicate her life to God, she cut her hair, disguised herself as a young man, changed her name to Juanico, and made her way to Galicia. Still in disguise, she joined a monastic order and spent five years working diligently within the monastery walls. It is unclear whether she remained a novice during this time or actually became a monk.

The story ends with Juanico deciding that she would rather be María again, confessing the truth of her identity to the abbot and leaving for Pontevedra where she would request admission into the Convent of Santa Clara in Pontevedra. Despite being informed of her previous identity as Juanico, the abbess welcomes María. Apparently, the townspeople also warmly welcomed her when they heard about the story. When Sister María de San Antonio died, she was buried in the Convent of the Clarisas.

Santuario de las Apariciones (Sanctuary of the Visions)

It may not be the most grandiose or aesthetically stimulating of the Pontevedra monuments, but the humble Sanctuary of the Visions is one of the most visited and venerated places in town.

This is where Lucía dos Santos, one of the three children who experienced the Fatima visions, stayed between 1925 and 1926, and where she had another vision of the Virgin Mary. At the time she was a member of the Dorothy Sisters Order and was living in Spain. She would later return in the 1940s to Portugal and join the better-known Carmelite Order till her death. And in case you are wondering, the vision happened in her cell on the second floor.

As in the case of the Basilica, the sanctuary is also off the Camino, on *Rúa Sor Lucía* in the historic quarter.

> Paio Gómez Chariño
>
> *The 13th century military hero, admiral and poet, Paio Gómez Chariño is buried in the Church of San Francisco amongst other notable citizens of Pontevedra. Chariño is also considered one of the founders of written Galician language thanks to his 'cantigas' (medieval poems that were sung).*
>
> *'As frores do meu amigo*
> *briosas van no navío,*
> *e vanse as frores*
> *d' aquí ben con meus amores*
> *idas son as frores.'*
>
> *(The flowers of my friend*
> *spirited sail away,*
> *and the flowers leave*
> *from here with my love*
> *the flowers have left.)*

Leaving Town

Leaving Pontevedra is as simple as following the well-marked yellow arrows that will navigate you across the historic quarter till you reach the River Lévez and the medieval Burgo Bridge. Once you cross the bridge, look out for the yellow arrows that take you down a side street (*Rúa A Santiña*), through the O Burgo quarter and before you know it out of Pontevedra.

Like in other towns along the Camino, pilgrims are pleasantly surprised that the way out of town is much nicer and less developed than the way in.

The Feast of Santiaguiño do Burgo

Every year, on the 24th of July, the little neighbourhood of O Burgo in Pontevedra celebrates its Feast Day. The local tradition believes that Saint James was passing through the area when he stopped for a rest by a farm where he was offered hospitality. Thankful, Saint James promised the farmers that they would be blessed every year with the first harvest of grapes and corn (even if corn did not arrive to Spain until 15 centuries later!).

Since the 19th century, a yearly procession has taken the image of Saint James from the Chapel of Santiago in O Burgo to Rúa A Santiña, 95 where the Couto Family has lived for generations. The Couto Family in turn honour the image by placing a bunch of grapes and some corncobs on the apostle's staff; and then inviting everyone to Galician empanada, soft-drinks and, of course, wine!

There is a small metal plaque commemorating this event at number 95 Rúa A Santiña, right on the Portuguese Camino as you leave Pontevedra

This stage takes you along quiet country lanes and trails through small vineyards and several scenic hamlets. The first half of the stage takes you through wooded areas while the second half opens up to the vineyards and farmland. Happily, this stage also offers several bars with pilgrim services (drinks and food), which appear as oases in an otherwise coffee-barren landscape. Before reaching Caldas de Reis you can make a short detour and visit the Río Barosa waterfalls, which are easy to get to and just off the Camino.

Don't mess with the locals

On his way back from Santiago, 15th century Czech pilgrim Baron Rosmithal was confronted by a mob of at least 100 peasants heavily armed. It is unclear from Rosmithal's account whether this was an attempted robbery or simply the locals seeking justice after a page in Rosmithal's party injured a local by accident with a stone as they were travelling to Santiago. The incident was serious enough for Rosmithal to describe in detail the exchange with the locals and the resolution of the problem. Again it is unclear if the problem was solved because the locals realised that, even though they outnumbered Rosmithal's party, the Czech's were well armed and possibly trained in fighting, or if it was because of Rosmithal's threats regarding the likely retribution in the case of an assault on a nobleman. The episode ends with Rosmithal's party safely continuing their journey.

Variante Espiritual (The Alternative Spiritual Route)

About two kilometres after leaving Pontevedra you will come to a panel indicating the possibility of leaving the classic route and continuing your Camino on the Alternative Spiritual Route.

This newly marked route takes you west towards the coast where you will follow the Arousa estuary northeast to Pontecesures and Padrón, where this route converges again with the Portuguese Camino. Tradition believes that Santiago sailed down the Arousa estuary, docking in Iria Flavia. Highlights of this route include the Monasteries of Poio and Armenteira, the historic town of Combarros, the castle ruins at Catoira, the views of the Arousa estuary and (if you do it) sailing up the estuary to Pontecesures and Padrón, just as Saint James did 2000 years ago!

Be warned that this route will add another 72 kilometres to your Camino.

Church of Santa María del Alba

The solemn and somewhat altered 16th century Church of Santa María, its cemetery and the impressive next-door 18th century rectory have always been closed when I have walked by.

However, the life-size sculpture of the late parish priest D. Juliám López Souto makes for a fun (and respectful) photo. Just after the church is another *cruceiro* marking the way.

Alba/Chapel of San Caetano

Yes, there is a chapel here, which is always closed. No, there is nothing else here apart from perhaps the most dangerous 500 metres on the whole Camino and a series of homes and warehouses. Unfortunately the Camino shares the shoulder with the oncoming traffic on an always very busy road. The main problem is that there really is no shoulder. The tiny 18th century Church of San Caetano manages to proudly standout, despite the road, bridge and continuous flow of vehicles. The even smaller statue of San Caetano encased in a scallop shell over the door is a friendly wink of the eye to the brave pilgrims that pass by.

Train track crossing

Because everybody loves trains and train tracks that you can actually walk on! You've been under these tracks twice already, now you get to walk on them and take that iconic photo of a *pilgrim walking on train tracks*.

San Amaro (or San Mauro) (Km57.5)

The first of the oases on today's stage magically appears as you gain the hill through the woods and enter the hamlet of San Mauro. Your bliss will then turn to disbelief when you discover that the little hamlet has two bars almost facing each other, *La Pousada del Peregrino* and *Don Pulpo* (yes, that's *Mr. Octopus*). I have had coffee at both and both were great (the coffee and the staff). In line with many of the other villages you have already walked through, San Mauro is rural but hardly picturesque.

Saint Amaro, Amarus, Mauro or Maurus

The hagiography and identity of Saint Amaro is often confused with Saint Mauro's, and to make matters even more confusing, both are widely venerated throughout Spain. However, as Saint Amaro fits the Camino story better and is associated with Galicia's Celtic roots, I am going to assume that the town of San Amaro (or San Mauro) is named after him (I have not been able to get a clear answer from any of the locals regarding the identity of the saint).

Saint Amaro was a 13th century French abbot and pilgrim who not only completed the pilgrimage to Santiago de Compostela but also decided to settle down in Castile, open a hospice for lepers and not return to France. However, Saint Amaro is also commonly associated with the legend of Saint Amaro the sailor, who decided to search for Paradise on Earth by sailing west into the unknown. His adventures, that closely resemble other Celtic and pagan myths about journeys into the unknown in search of other worlds, include sea monsters, female spirits, beautiful women, nuns, lost cities, deserted islands, time travel and finally Paradise itself.

It is unclear how the life of Saint Amaro the Sailor fits in with the life of Saint Amaro the Pilgrim.

Once you come off the San Amaro hill, the Camino stays flat all the way into Caldas de Reis. Hats and sunscreen may be in order if it is sunny as there will be little shade as you wander through the local vineyards.

Alfonso II the Chaste

A short note on Alfonso II, known as the Chaste as he did not have descendants and it is rumoured that his wife also died a virgin. He was first crowned king of Asturias in 783 although he was dethroned by his uncle that same year. Eight years later he was crowned king again reigning until his death in 842. His reign was characterised by numerous court intrigues and continuous military campaigns against or from the Emirate of Córdoba. He was also contemporary to Charlemagne with whom it appears he may have maintained contact.

During his reign the tomb of the Apostle Santiago was discovered and Alfonso II played an important role in the process of verification and initiating the pilgrimage you are now on. Indeed, he apparently travelled to the site of the discovery and built a church (present day Santiago de Compostela) becoming in this manner the first pilgrim of the Camino. Apart from chaste, Alfonso II was definitely an astute king. Through the discovery of the apostle's tomb he appropriated a thousand year old Celtic route that led to Finisterre (the end of the world) on the west coast in Galicia giving the route a new Christian meaning, as well as providing a pretext for a steady influx of pilgrims and settlers from the rest of Europe over the next centuries who would play an important role in securing the territories that were gradually conquered from the Muslims.

A Eira Bar

It should be open, and if it is, it's the only food or drink options for several kilometres.

Waterfalls at Río Barroso (Km 51)

The Camino briefly intersects with the N-550 here, continuing for about 500 metres on the left shoulder of the highway. If you cross the highway and make a short detour from the Camino, half a kilometre down the side road are the Río Barroso Waterfalls. This tourist attraction is well indicated from the highway and the waterfalls are worth the effort, if you have the time and energy. In the summer months there is a small café and toilets by the falls. There is also another small café facing the N-550 (and the Camino), right where you would cross the highway if you have decided to visit the waterfalls.

Towns and Parroquias

The administrative organisation of Galicia is the following (starting from the smallest unit and moving to the largest): parroquias (parishes), municipios (municipalities/towns), comarcas (counties) and provincias (provinces). The four provinces in Galicia make up the Autonomous Community of Galicia.

Only the municipalities/towns and provinces have political representation with mayors and provincial presidents elected every four years. The 'parroquias' and 'comarcas' are traditional administrative regions and may share cultural, social and economic ties. In fact, each municipality/town groups several 'parroquias', and each province groups several 'comarcas'.

So don't feel confused when you're walking through a town and discover that it has a different name than what your guidebook says, as it may be the parroquia name.

The last kilometres into Caldas may feel like they go on forever if it's a hot and sunny (or cold and rainy) day as all the shade you have previously enjoyed at the beginning of the stage disappears. Most pilgrims I have spoken to find the walk into Caldas engaging enough, especially in the late summer when the grapes are almost ready for picking, but at the same time arduous and long.

Note that there is a bit of highway shoulder walking that is unavoidable after the waterfalls. However, most of the section is on trails away from the highway, even if the Camino intersects it on a couple occasions.

Thankfully Caldas de Reis greets weary pilgrims with one of the best surprises on the whole Camino: free soothing hot water feet baths!

Aguardiente

At some point on your walk across Galicia you may be offered aguardiente (literally, fire water). Galicians take pride in their aguardiente, and in almost every bar and restaurant I have eaten at in Galicia, the bottle brought out clearly indicated that it was distilled at home and not bought at a supermarket. Galicians typically drink it after a meal, as a digestive, although they may drink it at other times as well. Apparently the closest equivalent to aguardiente that may be understandable to foreigners is grappa, although I prefer how a colleague of mine refers to it as jet fuel. It is a very alcoholic beverage (easily 60% per volume) and delivers a very miserable day after if drunk in excess. Aguardiente is produced from grape remains, basically the stuff not used to make wine.

Most of the pilgrims that walk with me prefer the fruity flavoured aguardientes (if the liquid is clear like water, you know it's the real deal, everything else that is coloured is flavoured). Aguardiente is also used to make the touristy-but-lots-of-fun Queimada.

Queimada

A Queimada is a punch like drink prepared in a clay pot with aguardiente and flavoured with different spices and coffee beans. Typically an incantation is recited during its preparation (when the Queimada is lit and the alcohol slowly burns on the surface of the punch) so as to give the Quiemada the power to ward off evil spirits (copies of the spell can be found everywhere on Internet).

I doubt that the locals prepare Queimadas in the intimacy of their homes; however, it is definitely part of Galician identity and always a favourite with tourists and guests, both Spanish and foreigners.

Briallos

Unless you are stopping or staying at the pilgrims' hostel, there really isn't much else in this little village. The Camino intersects briefly with the N-550 here and then quickly takes you back into wine country through what feels like people's back gardens at times.

Tivo (Km 46.8)

The serene little village of Tivo sits just outside Caldas de Reis and boasts a pretty fountain, an upright *cruceiro* and a friendly hostel and bar (also with great coffee!).

Caldas de Reis (Km 44)

Entering Caldas de Reis

After a long day you will finally enter Caldas de Reis on the N-550, which as in other towns, becomes the main road as it crosses town. Before the bridge that crosses the River Umia taking you into town, you will have left the interesting 18th century Church of Santa María with its Romanesque west door to your left.

Once over the bridge, take your first left and head straight for the thermal footbath. The thermal waters face the main town square and the church, and where the magnificent palm trees that crowd the square remind us as that you have reached the last oasis of the stage.

PADRÓN 26

Chapel of Santiaguiño

Ulla River crossing

Pontecesures 27.8

San Miguel de Valga 33

AP-9 crossing

Carracedo 40

Careful when crossing here

CALDAS DE REIS 44

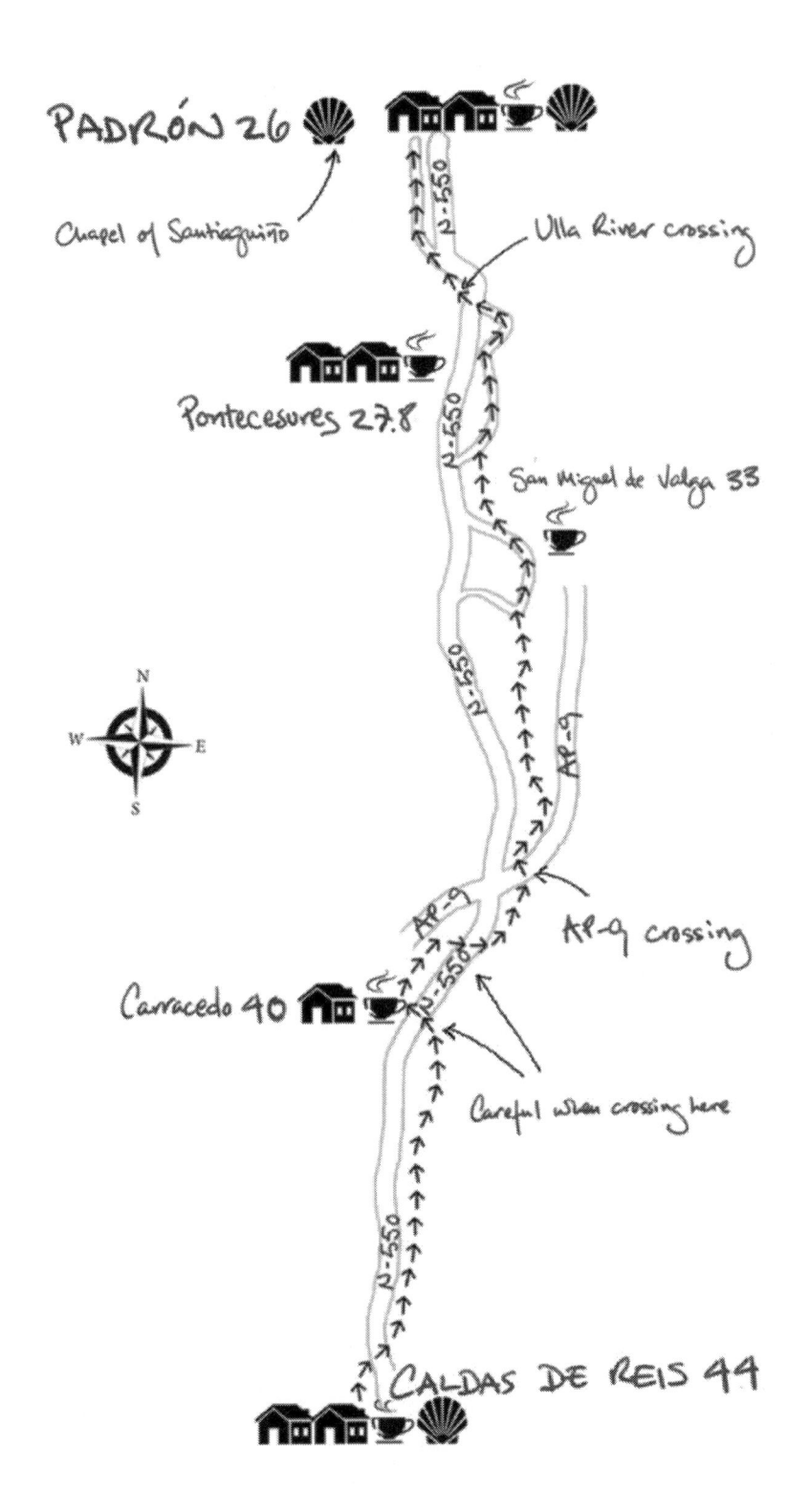

STAGE 5. Caldas de Reis to Padrón (18.5 km)

This stage is a bit more challenging than yesterday's, as the first part of the day takes you up and over another hill with some sections of steep downhill until you reach the River Sar valley and enter Padrón. Your efforts will be rewarded on the more strenuous first part with some amazing trails through wooded areas, vineyards and a couple scenic towns.

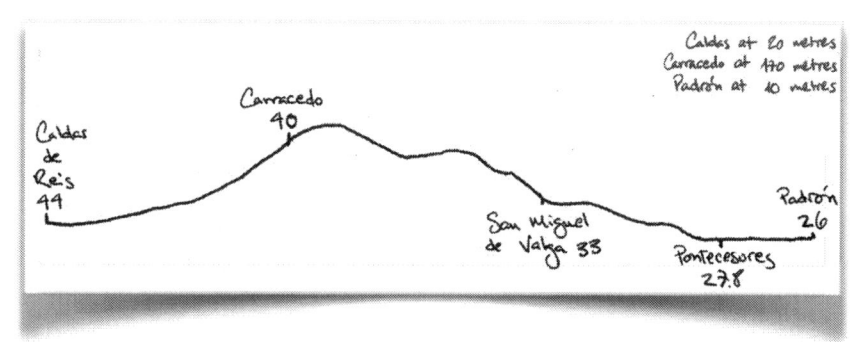

On this stage you will walk through the plain ugly Pontecesures before reaching the intriguing and pretty town of Padrón. Remember that it was in Padrón where *it all began*, so for many pilgrims this stage is a significant one, perhaps only second to the arrival in Santiago de Compostela.

Caldas de Reis (Km 44)

Caldas de Reis (or just *Caldas* as the locals call it) has always been and perhaps will always be associated with its thermal hot springs. And what better place to set up camp or even build a town than where you can get free hot water with purported therapeutic properties? The Romans knew this, the Galician gentry knew this, even the celebrated 15th century pilgrim Hieronymus Münzer knew this, when the first thing he did according to his diary on arrival to Caldas was soak his feet.

The historical accounts

Confalonieri mentions that the locals fish trout in the river but does not stop for lunch. He was not too impressed with the town, describing it as 'a small place or a town without walls, with houses and streets in the Galician style, and 200 or 300 hearths'. Confalonieri, always an admirer of bridges, says that the town 'has a good bridge before and one after, and its called the Caldas Bridge'. And there are indeed two bridges in Caldas that you will cross as you enter and leave town. Engrossed in his bridge spotting, he ignores the thermal springs.

Münzer on the other hand was intrigued by the springs but (like Confalonieri a century later) not by the town. He describes how he tried the 'thermal and sulphurous waters', which he found to be 'excellent and as warm as the ones in Padua, near Torino'. However, he ends up complaining about having to use a hole dug in the ground to bathe as the 'townspeople are so negligent that they have not built even the smallest building, not even bath areas'. Thankfully, this has changed.

The history of Caldas de Reis dates back to Roman times when it was a popular stop, for obvious reasons, on the *Vía XIX*. It was at the *Mansio de Aquis Celenis*, where *patricians* (wealthy) and *plebeians* (poor) would not only soak their feet but also make their rounds of the *frigidarium* (cold pool) and *caldarium* (hot pool). Unfortunately, the art of bathing and cleansing oneself declined considerably during the middle ages, and it wouldn't be until the 19th century when Caldas de Reis would be put back on the map as a spa resort town for the Galician gentry. You can still visit the 19th century spas of Dávila and Acuña in town where you will be provided with all the amenities expected in the 21st century.

And if soaking your weary feet is enough for you, then pop them into the public hot spring pool that is just a couple blocks from the main square.

Apart from its hot springs, Caldas has also been an important pit stop on the Camino for weary pilgrims. The proud 19th century Church of *Santo Tomás Becket* (yes, that's Saint Thomas Becket) stands in the main square in town surrounded by imposing palm trees. The church is named in honour of the English saint who stopped here on his way to Santiago. Likewise, you will have passed by the once-Romanesque and now a mismatch of styles, Church of *Santa María*, as you came into town and before you crossed the river. All the bridges in town have Roman foundations and have been around since then.

Ugly Spanish towns

I believe a word must be said about Spanish towns.

Although Spain has its share of very pretty and picturesque towns, you will have noted as you cross Galicia that there appears to be somewhat of an overrepresentation of ugly towns. Ugly is understood as: a) towns lacking in character or aesthetic harmony, b) that have torn completely (or almost completely) down their historic centres in favour of depersonalised rows of cloned buildings, c) that have sacrificed their architectural heritage in favour of the functionality of modern buildings, d) that appear to only understand the use of brick or cement as construction materials, e) that don't make you pull out your camera.

Most pilgrims I lead tend to exercise diplomacy when bringing up this subject, afraid they might hurt local (perhaps even my) feelings. But the truth is that these towns are just plain ugly.

Underdeveloped Spain (in contrast to northern Europe) came out of the Spanish Civil War perhaps even more underdeveloped (both economically as well intellectually). However, development and urban migration eventually caught up with Spain and in the late '50s the first real estate agents appeared, visionaries who saw how to make a lot of money through lax or inexistent laws (or government corruption) and distorted ideas of modernity and functionality. By the seventies, most of the larger towns throughout Spain had suffered the impact of these brave new ideas, that basically consisted in tearing down old village homes (that were too costly to maintain and required extensive refurbishing to provide modern amenities), and building depersonalised apartment buildings.

This trend has found new vigour during the last twenty years with widespread speculation (and corruption) in real estate and construction, creating the chaotic sprawls that now grace these towns.

Toponymy of Caldas de Reis

There is no intrigue in this one. *Caldas* means *hot thermal springs* and *de Reis* means *of Kings*. Put the two parts together and we get *The Kings' Hot Thermal Springs*. The *kings* part most likely refers to Alfonso VII of León, who was born here in the 12th century, after which the town began to be called *Caldas de Rex*.

Leaving Town

Leaving Caldas de Reis is straightforward. Follow the Camino across the square leaving the church and palm trees to your right and head down the small street *Rúa Real*, which will cross a larger street (ignore it) and eventually cross the River Bermaña over a Roman/medieval bridge. *Rúa Real* becomes *Rúa San Roque*, veering slightly to your right, and *Rúa San Roque* intersects with the N-550. Don't worry, there are lots of arrows! The Camino then follows the N-550 for a couple hundred metres and branches off to the right into the surrounding fields.

It's a pretty uphill walk through mainly wooded areas and along trails and quiet roads as you leave Caldas. To the right you may be able to make out the small Bermaña River through the dozens of small vegetable plots and vineyards that dot the valley. The Camino then intersects with the N-550 at the top of the hill and as you enter the village of Carracedo. The Camino crosses the highway and takes you in and through town only to take you out of town a bit further down the hill where it crosses the N-550 again returning to the right side of the road. You may be tempted to shave off a couple metres of the Camino and just stay on the highway, which would be a mistake as Carracedo is a pretty town with an old flavour feel to it and a lovely church.

The stretch between Carracedo and San Miguel de Valga is again mostly on trails with spots of small paved roads. You will however walk alongside (you are actually a bit above it and on the other side of a fence) a major expressway (which you will cross) for at least a kilometre or more. Apart from this unavoidable scar on the Camino, you will also be rewarded with more farmland hiking, with lots of grapes and an amazing couple of kilometres on a forest trail as you make your way downhill to San Miguel de Valga.

The last section of the stage takes you into the town of Pontecesures with its smoke bellowing sawmill and furniture factory, and through the urban sprawl of Padrón. And just when you are about to give up hope, the historic quarter of Padrón greets you with welcoming arms, shaded avenues and a fresh cup of coffee, and you are time-warped back to the year AD 44.

Carracedo (Km 40)

After a short uphill walk through mainly wooded areas and farmland you will arrive to the town of Carracedo, which sits along the N-550. You may or may not require it, but the friendly bar *El Espelón* facing the highway and just off the Camino is a great place to stop and perhaps grab a *café con leche*. Unlike many other bars along the Portuguese

Camino, the couple that run the bar actually appear to enjoy the arrival of pilgrims and rush out their stamp with a big smile. They also have a small side room where they let pilgrims write messages or just their names, on the wall and ceiling! And no worries if you don't have a marker or pen, the good people at the bar will provide you with one.

And if you can spot a Survival Guide's Message, take a photo and email it to me and I'll send you a copy of the other Survival Guide, for the French Camino ☺).

Carracedo is a pretty town with narrow allies and stone buildings. And in the middle of town and right on the Camino you'll walk by the Church of Santa Mariña. This church is a beautiful example of 18th century Galician religious architecture with its solemn bell tower overlooking the vale below. Facing the church there is also a *cruceiro* missing its horizontal arm, the remains of the old rectory and an amazing example of an *hórreo* (traditional corncrib). Unfortunately I have not been able to visit the inside of the church yet.

Santa Mariña (Saint Marina)

Saint Mariña is a popular saint venerated across Galicia. Tradition believes that she lived and died a martyr by beheading in the second century AD.

Up to here you have a classic martyrdom story, but in the case of Santa Mariña things get a bit messy right at her birth. Apparently the wife of a Roman governor in Hispania had given birth to nine girls (yes, you read right, nine) while her husband was away doing what Roman governors do and afraid that she would be accused of adultery (there may have been grounds for this accusation although the story does not clarify this), she decides to drown all nine girls ordering her servant Sila to do the evil deed. Sila, who is a Christian, decides to disobey her mistress and saves the children by finding foster homes for them where they are brought up as Christians.

Years later, when they are adolescents, Mariña and her sisters are accused of being Christians and taken to the governor (her father), who incarcerates them until they renounce their faith. He has already found out (although we do not know how) that these are his own daughters and tempts them with a comfortable pagan life under his protection. The sisters refuse his offers and manage to escape the prison, only to be caught again, tortured and executed.

In the case of Santa Mariña (the story has different variations), she was charged and imprisoned by a Roman suitor and soldier under her father's command. As she rejected him he decided to retaliate and once imprisoned he tortured her with the following methods: burning her feet with sweltering iron rods, tying weights to her hands and feet and dropping her into a well, tearing her flesh off with hooks and incinerating her alive in a furnace. She was saved by divine intervention in all of the above cases. Fed up, the soldier decided to simply behead her, and that worked.

Just before you come off the Valga hills and out of the forest you will see a sign to your left pointing to Bar Los Camioneros, with pilgrim services, very early opening hours (5 am?) and a stamp! Truth be said, I have not had a chance to check this bar out. However, just in case you were wondering, Los Camioneros translates as The Truck Drivers, so I am sure they serve a very strong coffee, and I am intrigued about their pilgrim stamp.

San Miguel de Valga (Km 33)

Once off the hill you will approach San Miguel de Valga along a country lane. San Miguel is a quiet little village with a pretty 18th century church (similar to the one you saw in Carracedo) and cemetery, another rectory, a *cruceiro* and a convenient bar and small supermarket (all in one). After San Miguel, the Camino gradually becomes pavement and streets, all the way into Padrón.

The battle at Casal do Erigio

Near the expressway crossing, just off the Camino, another battle between Napoleon's troops and Spanish irregular forces took place. On the 27th of April of 1809, Spanish forces made up primarily of armed locals led by military hero Pablo Murillo and, after a brutal clash, forced Napoleon's troops to retreat back to Pontecesures. A commemorative plaque by the church states that Napoleon's troops outnumbered the locals five-to-one, and that they lost 300 men. Indeed, even the Duke of Wellington was so impressed by the feat that he is believed to have said during the Spanish War of Independence: 'Spaniards, strive to imitate the incomparable Galicians'.

To commemorate the battle, the nearby Chapel of Nosa Señora da Saúde was erected.

The follow up to this battle was the decisive Battle of Pontesampaio (see Stage 3)

La Bella Otero (The Beautiful or 'Belle' Otero)

Agustina Otero was born in the municipality of Valga in 1868. After a dramatic childhood that included working as a maid in Santiago de Compostela at the age of 10, being raped at around that same age and escaping to Portugal with her boyfriend at the age of 14, she commenced a successful career as a dancer, actress and courtesan.

She modelled her career around the character of La Bella Otero, an exotic Spanish Romani from the south of Spain. By the turn of the century she was associated with men from the highest social classes across Europe, and was thoughtfully choosing her lovers.

Her Traviata-like lifestyle led her to the bedchambers of kings, aristocrats, socialites and countless other admirers. Likewise, legends talk of several men committing suicide and challenging others to duels after being rejected by her. By the early 20th century she had retired with a fortune of 25 million dollars, which was really a lot of money back then.

La Bella Otero died in Nice, alone and in poverty at the age of 96 after enjoying years of excess during the 'années folles' and up to the Second World War.

La Bella Otero is credited with having said that 'Women have one mission in life: to be beautiful. When one gets old, one must learn how to break mirrors.' This quote is reprehensible by our current sociocultural standards; however, in context, it does appear (sadly) to have suited her choice of life.

Pontecesures (Km 27.8)

As you cross the bridge, you may find it difficult to believe that this town was once a prized port of strategic and commercial importance for Romans and battling medieval warlords. Most pilgrims will now associate Pontecesures with the gargantuan factory that straddles the opposite side of the river and the busy motor traffic on the bridge. Perhaps this is the essence of the town, what Pontecesures has always been: transit and trade; and that even if the forms have changed with modernity, the underlying spirit remains the same. Indeed, even the origin of the town's name appears to be linked to its bridge (*ponte*) and local economy (*cesures* may derive from the Latin word *censere*, meaning *to tax*).

Two factories

You can't help but see one of them, but there's another one, which is less conspicuous. So in case you are wondering:

The large factory by the river belching out smoke is a sawmill and furniture factory (Finsa), one of the leading companies in Galicia and more importantly, employs over 3.000 people (across Spain) and apparently has been around since 1931.

The other one, the one you don't see, is a bit *sweeter*, as it's a major Nestlé factory. This smaller factory faces the sawmill on the opposite side of the river, and, if condensed milk is your thing, then this is your place, as they are Nestlé's producers for this product in all of Europe. The factory has been here since 1939.

So next time you are lounging on a sofa on the Camino and sipping a *café bombón* (espresso with condensed milk), you just might recall your walk through Pontecesures.

An abbreviated history of Pontecesures

As you cross Pontecesures, you may find it hard to believe that it has had an important past that dates back to Roman times. What is now a patchwork of functional residential areas and industrial estates (and a very large factory) was once one of the main seaports in this part of Galicia.

Pontecesures was considered, until the 20th century, the *port of Santiago* as this was the port of reference for trade to and from the city. Even before, in Roman times, Pontecesures was a port of reference (with an important bridge) for the region. In the 12th and 13th centuries its shipyards would produce the ships that would patrol the Galician coasts protecting pilgrims coming from Engand and merchants from Moorish pirates and Viking raiders.

The River Ulla and crossing into A Coruña

As you cross the once-Roman-now-modern N-550 bridge over the River Ulla, you will be leaving the province of Pontevedra, which you will have literally crossed from south to north, and entering the province of A Coruña. The River Ulla flows into the Arosa Estuary and the Altlantic Ocean. Santiago de Compostela is in the province of A Coruña.

The Order of Santiago

Similar to the Medieval Order of the Knights Templar (without the vow of poverty and chastity), the Order of Santiago (emblem of a red cross that recalls an upside down sword) was a religious and military order established in present Spain in the XII century (although some would like to believe it was founded in 844 just after the Battle of Clavijo, where Santiago appeared on his horse, sword in hand; makes sense). They operated mainly in northern Spain against Muslim forces, protecting pilgrims on the Camino. The Order, once its military and religious factions united, managed a network of hospices on the Camino, all the way from the Pyrenees to Santiago.

Once Spain was united the Order gradually became an elitist association. In other words, anyone who was anybody in 17th century Spain sought to belong to this exclusive club. Velázquez, the court painter and author of the Meninas, was knighted as a knight of the Order of Santiago only after the mediation of several influential people in court. Indeed, he had to prove that he was a nobleman and son and grandson of noblemen, and that the blood in his family had been pure (requirements to be knighted) for three generations (no Muslim or Jewish relatives). Surprisingly, the Order considered painting as not working with one's hands for a living, another of the requirements.

The Order of Santiago was dissolved twice during both Spanish republican governments. It has since been reinstated and is now a civil association with a strong religious and aristocratic reminiscence.

Herbón

Just before you cross the Ulla River into the province of A Coruña, you may see arrows indicating a possible detour to the Monastery of San Antonio in the village of Hebrón.

The fairly large complex makes for an interesting visit if you are not pressed for time, and there is even a pilgrims' hostel and more than ten hectares of wooded grounds by the river that are guaranteed to meet your meditation requirements. Run by the Franciscans, the order has been here since the 14th century, although almost nothing remains from this era. Perhaps the monastery's main call to fame is that it was here that the Franciscans first cultivated their Padrón Peppers (see next chapter) brought all the way from America.

Be warned that this detour will add another six kilometres to your Camino.

Padrón (Km 26)

Entering Padrón

After crossing the bridge at Pontecesures, the Camino takes you along the banks of the River Sar, which you will follow into town. Unfortunately the surroundings do not improve much as Padrón has sprawled chaotically towards Pontecesures to the extent that you will not really know when you have left or entered either one.

Just before you enter Padrón city centre you will have to cross what look like a very large parking lot (which it is), where the weekly local market is held and which is poorly marked with arrows. Once having crossed the parking lot you will reach a sycamore tree avenue (also poorly marked) alongside the river, the *Rúa Castelao*, that leads the way into town. *Rúa Castelao* is flanked on the south side by an unusual monument of Spain's last Nobel Literature Prize laureate Camilo José Cela (note the unusual and intriguing large balls) and on the north side with a more graceful monument of Galicia's most famous poet and one of the greatest poets in Spanish history, Rosalía de Castro. Both are associated closely to Padrón. The Church of Santiago is at the end of the sycamore avenue and the Camino continues on from there. The Camino does not cross the bridge.

The Spanish Civil War in Galicia

Galicia was one of the few regions that supported almost unconditionally the fascist insurrection. The fact that Franco was from Ferrol in Galicia may have helped to rally military and social support. The Catholic Church, which officially sided with the fascists, also had a much stronger influence in rural Galicia than in other parts of Spain. Likewise, foreign ideas, such as socialism and women's rights would have been much more alien to your average Galician farmer in 1936. In this manner Galicia became a fascist stronghold during the Civil war and, although there were summary executions and thousands of detainees, there were no major battles fought in Galicia.

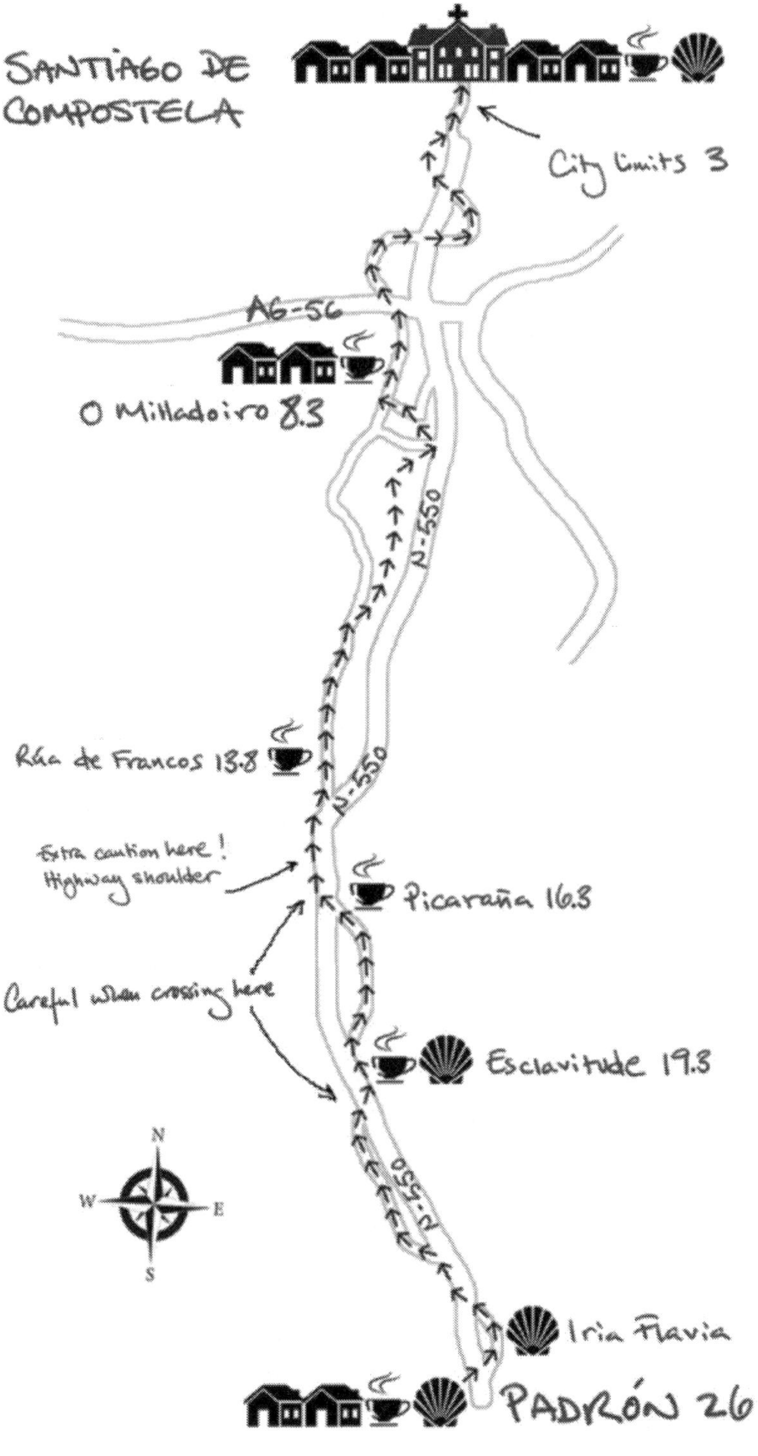
SANTIAGO DE COMPOSTELA
City limits 3
AG-56
O Milladoiro 8.3
N-550
Rúa de Francos 13.8
N-550
Extra caution here! Highway shoulder
Picaraña 16.3
Careful when crossing here
Esclavitude 19.3
N-550
Iria Flavia
PADRÓN 26
N
W
E
S

STAGE 6. Padrón to Santiago de Compostela (23.5 km)

The final stage of your Camino is similar to the previous ones, with a mix of quiet paved roads, trails, the ubiquitous N-550, and a handful of interesting historic features. It is also long, so depending on what time you leave you will either be having a late lunch in Santiago or checking into your accommodation for a late siesta (or celebrating). The last couple of kilometres are on city sidewalks.

Padrón (Km 26)

For Catholic pilgrims Padrón has a special significance, as this is where they celebrate Santiago in life, where his apostolic mission began and where he preached his first sermons attempting to convert the local pagans. Indeed, a much-overlooked fact is that Santiago arrived twice to Padrón by boat, once alive and once dead. In this manner, 1200 years of pilgrimages to Santiago cemented in Camino tradition has made the celebration of his death and his burial place in Santiago de Compostela the centre of the Santiago story. But it's here, in Padrón (actually, at next door Iria Flavia to be more precise), where it *all began*.

Padrón is now a small town that has sprawled out along the ever present N-550, too far from Santiago to become a suburb, and too close for it to become a commercial reference for the region. In many ways the town appears to be unaware of its importance in the Camino story, or even of the momentum the Portuguese Camino has gathered over the last years. The Church of Santiago is still painfully hard to visit closing at inconvenient times, the Santiago-related sights are poorly marked, I have still to find the tourist booth (conveniently off the

Camino) open, accommodation is surprisingly limited, and the bars appear to cater more to the locals than pilgrims.

The small town of Padrón is also associated with two of Spain's most renowned and read authors, Rosalía de Castro and Camilo José Cela.

> *The historical accounts*
>
> *Rosmithal described Padrón as the place where 'the Apostle of Santiago failed, as after one year of preaching he was only able to convert two men to the faith in Christ'. These are harsh words in my opinion, true according to tradition, but harsh all the same. In town they visited the Chapel of Santiaguiño, 'they saw on a hill that overlooked the town a certain church standing in the place of the Apostle's preaching, close to a cave where the saint sought refuge from the pagans' stones'.*
>
> *It is unlikely that they saw a church at the top of the hill overlooking the town as Padrón would not be visible from the hill. In any case, it appears that they did indeed make it to the top of the hill and visited the place where Santiago is believed to have preached and lived while in Padrón. It is possible that Rosmithal could have seen a chapel in this place as the current one, many times redone, appears to have been built in the 15th century. As for the cave, I have not been able to find one yet.*
>
> *Confalonieri's account is much more concise. He simply states that the town has '200 homes, with a very beautiful bridge with 17 arches', and that he felt like he was looking at the Tiber in Rome (he must have been a bit homesick).*
>
> *Münzer had a bit more to say, describing Padrón as an old city previously called Iria. He did a full tour of the town, similar to the one you can do now. He went first to the Church of Santiago, then to the riverside where Santiago's boat moored and finally up to the top of the hill where he visited the chapel and the miraculous spring, which they drank from finding it 'smooth and light, which was very restoring'.*

The sights

As you enter town along the river, you will undoubtedly see a very large church on the hill to your left overlooking the town. This is the *Convento del Carmen* (Convent of the Carmen). The church and convent date from the 18th century and you can only visit the church, which has an annoying tendency to be closed every time I go up there.

Likewise, if you look carefully, on the left side of the river and down by the riverbank near the bridge, there is a replica of the *Pedrón*. So if the Church of Santiago is closed or you just want a selfie with the cleat that Santiago's boot was moored to, then you might consider crossing to the other side. There is also the interesting 16th century *Fuente del Carmen* (Fountain of the Carmen) on the other side of the bridge, which depicts the conversion of Queen Lupa to Christianity and the arrival of Santiago's remains to Padrón. The fountain houses the statue of the *Virgen de de los Dolores* (literally the Virgin of the Pains), who is apparently the person who can alleviate childbirth delivery pains.

Church of Santiago

Most pilgrims that have walked with me have found the Church of Santiago (and indeed most of Padrón) somewhat disappointing. Long gone are the Romanesque and Gothic churches that once heralded pilgrims as they went by, and it is doubtful that the current neoclassic-inspired 19th century church will make the cover of your Camino de Santiago photo album when you return home. Apart from the religious significance of the place, the most interesting aspect of the church is that the relic of the *Pedrón* can still be venerated under the altar.

The Church of Santiago is found at the end of the riverside promenade into town. The Camino does not cross the bridge that is on the left of the church, but goes around the front of the church and then through town.

Chapel of Santiaguiño and Santiaguiño area

Few are the pilgrims that make it up to the Chapel of Santiaguiño at the top of the hill. The 132 large steps that take you up to chapel are a powerful reason to reconsider making this excursion. However, this is also perhaps the most moving and inspiring place in the whole Padrón district and well worth the effort. The stairs that take you up can be found to the right of the *Fuente del Carmen* after crossing the bridge. However, your best bet is to double-check with a local.

At the top of the hill you will find a pretty recreational area, fit with picnic tables, barbecues and lots of shade. You will also find the quaint little Chapel of Santiaguiño, a monument to Santiago's first sermons in Spain and a fountain of spring water. Tradition believes that this is the place where Santiago took refuge from the locals' wrath at the bottom of the hill, where he preached his first sermons and where he made water come out of a rock by hitting it three times with his staff (that's the current fountain).

Every year, on the Feast of Santiago (25th of July), the Apostle is venerated here. There is also lots of drinking, eating and dancing.

Toponymy of Padrón

The town is named after the rock that served as a cleat to which the boat that brought Santiago's corpse back from Palestine was moored. Rock in Spanish is *piedra*, a large rock would be a *pedrón*, and *pedrón* became *padrón*. In the case of Padrón, the original *pedrón* might well have been a Roman milestone from the Roman *Vía XIX*.

Leaving Town

Leaving Padrón is fairly straightforward. You will follow the arrows through the unremarkable backstreets of town, walking more or less parallel to the N-550 to your right. Thankfully this section is not long and it is well marked.

Almost as soon as you leave town through the backstreets of Padrón you will intersect with the N-550 and the village and Church of Iria Flavia. Another easy five kilometres down the Camino will take you to the equally impressive Church of Esclavitude. After Esclavitude you will commence the progressive ascent of the last hill on the Camino.

Padrón Peppers

Os pementos de Padrón, uns pican e outros non (Padrón peppers, some are hot and others aren't). And that is exactly what can happen when you eat these addictive delicacies. The good news is that only one in every hundred is hot, at least that's what the locals say.

Padrón peppers have been grown along the banks of the rivers Ulla and Sar in Padrón since the Jesuits introduced them 400 years ago, and they have now become a signature dish, not only for the local region but for all of Galicia. The small peppers are usually served fried or roasted with a dash of rock salt.

The surprising literary heritage of Padrón

A Nobel Prize in Literature and Spain's most famous female poet are both closely associated to Padrón. Not bad for a small town with a current population of under 9000.

Rosalía de Castro was born in Santiago in 1837, but spent her childhood in Padrón where she would die 48 years later. She is considered one of the leading figures in Spanish poetry, and one of the first writers to publish in Galician and not in Castilian (Spanish). She is buried in the Pantheon of Illustrious Galicians, in the Convent of Santo Domingo de Bonaval in Santiago. The following is an extract from her last book of poems, 'A Orillas del Sar' (On the banks of the Sar):

> El viajero, rendido y cansado,
> que ve del camino la línea escabrosa
> que aún le resta que andar, anhelara,
> deteniéndose al pie de la loma,
> de repente quedar convertido
> en pájaro o fuente,
> en árbol o en roca.

*(The traveller, exhausted and tired,
that sees the abrupt route of the path
that he still has to walk, yearns,
stopping at the foot of the hill,
to suddenly become
a bird or fountain,
a tree or rock.)*

Spain's last Nobel Prize of Literature laureate was Camilo José Cela. Cela was born in Iria Flavia (Padrón) in 1916 and died in 2002. He was awarded the Nobel Prize in 1989. Cela was a controversial figure, openly expressing his politically conservative views and his admiration and support for Franco's regime. He never shied from the fact that he had enlisted as a soldier on the Nationalist side during the Spanish Civil War. Apparently Cela's last words were:

'¡Viva Iria Flavia!' (Hail Iraia Flavia!).

There are monuments to both writers at either end of the treed promenade in town. While Rosalia's is graceful in a classic way, Cela's does a pretty good job of describing his character.

Iria Flavia

Iria Flavia has been around since Roman times, and this was the town where Santiago started his mission in Roman Hispania. This was also the seat of Bishop Teodomiro, who played an active role in the discovery of Santiago's tomb in 813. Indeed, Iria Flavia was the centre of the Catholic Church in Galicia until the rise to stardom of Santiago de Compostela in the 9th century.

Unfortunately, the rather large-but-plain church does not do justice to the importance Iria Flavia has played throughout history, nor is really anything left of the primitive temples.

The Camino crosses the N-550 just before the church and wanders off into the residential area of Iria Favia behind the church and not along the N-550.

Clubs

Spaniards and foreigners often get confused with the use of the word club *(as in a discotheque). What you probably understand is precisely that, a place where you go to dance and have a drink; a Spaniard understands: a brothel (drinks are also available). So if you do feel like getting dirty on the dance floor, you might want to consider using the Spanish term:* discoteca.

As for those dodgy looking buildings you may see along the highway or on the outskirts of towns with a large luminous Club sign, those are... yep, you guessed it).

The Camino soon intersects the N-550 after leaving Iria Flavia, and you will be walking along the side of this busy road again for a kilometre. This unsavoury part of the Camino will take you across a very large roundabout, and by the large tour-group Hotel Scala. Fortunately there are several bars along this section. Thankfully, the Camino does not continue along the N-550 all the way to Esclavitude but abruptly makes a left turn and takes you down into the fields and through the small villages that have astonishingly survived the pressure of the surrounding uncontrolled urban development. Thus, it's a very pretty and relaxed walk through vineyards, past people's homes and gardens and through tiny hamlets that have fused together with quaint names such as Porta dos Mariños, Tarrío and O Vilar, until you reach Esclavitude and the N-550 again. Please note that once you leave the N-550, pilgrim services disappear with it.

Esclavitude (Km 19.3)

You will approach Esclavitude following the train tracks and from behind a very large flourmill. The Camino then converges with the N-550 just before the very imposing, and very awkwardly placed, 19th century Church of Esclavitude (usually closed). There are a couple bars facing the road; I particularly like the tapas and service at Casa Eduardo, that's the one facing the church with the large parking area (use the crosswalk). Thankfully you will leave Esclavitude on a lane taking you behind the church and not on the N-550.

Perhaps the story behind Esclavitude (in English, literally *slavery*) is a bit more engaging than the town and church themselves. Apparently a very sick pilgrim in the 18th century prayed to the Virgin Mary to cure

109

his sickness and drank from the fountain that is still there in front of the church. The Virgin Mary interceded and he was cured. In gratitude, the pilgrim donated all his worldly possessions to build a sanctuary to the Virgin Mary (a smaller one than the one now) as she had saved him from the *slavery* of his illness. His literal words were: *"¡Gracias, Virxe, que me libraches da escravitude do meu mal!"* (Thank you, Virgin, for freeing me from the slavery of my illness!).

The *Virgen de Esclavitude* is venerated every 8th of September.

Areal/Picaraña (Km 16.3)

The Camino joins the N-550 for the last time in Picaraña, where there are a couple of friendly bars, a very large nightclub of dubious nature, a small industrial estate and a couple of cheap hotels. As you leave Picaraña, walking along the side of the N-550 and facing the traffic, you will see a small road that makes a hard left just before the bar/restaurant *Xantares Galegos*. About 300 metres down this quiet road you will see arrows pointing to the right into a wooded area. You then will follow a trail through this wooded area until you come out at Faramello.

Faramello

The hamlet of Faramello stands out for two reasons: first, this is where you will say good-bye for the last time to Highway N-550 (thank goodness!); and secondly, because of the outstanding, albeit usually overlooked, *Pazo de Faramello*.

The *Pazo de Faramello* is a 2.000 square metre, 18th century manor home with 13 hectares of gardens and woodland along the Río Tinto. This *pazo* was once the summer home of the Spanish monarch Alonso XIII (the great-grandfather of our current Spanish king), as well as the commercial and economic heart of the surrounding district. As a curiosity, apparently the Lord of Faramellos is the only person who holds the honour of being allowed to ride his horse into the Cathedral of Santiago; none have though. The estate can be visited although reservations are mandatory.

Unfortunately, the Camino no longer traverses the estate but goes around it following the quiet country lanes rather than the river.

Rúa de Francos (Km 13.8)

After a pleasant stroll you will arrive at the small village of *Rúa de Francos* (the village is called 'Street of the French'), which I am assuming was named after Napoleon's troops and not French pilgrims. Rúa de Francos has a simple church, an interesting *cruceiro* and a hostel with a bar that serves life-saving coffee. Some of your last stretches on dirt trails through wooded areas happen between this town and Milladoiro.

> **Queen Lupa's Castle**
>
> At Rúa de Francos you can consider visiting the remains of legendary Queen Lupa's castle. The castle is actually the not-so-impressive remains of a Celtic castro at the top of the nearby hill. This detour would add another 2.5 kilometres to your stage (and another difficult hill.
>
> Just in case you do not remember, and in a nutshell, Queen Lupa played a central part in the Santiago story as she was the ruler who received Santiago's disciples when they arrived with his remains and was asked for permission to bury him in her realm. As a good evil pagan, she sent them off to get eaten by a nearby dragon. However, the disciples were saved, she converted to Christianity and granted them permission to bury him in current Santiago de Compostela. So technically she decided where we would end up walking to 2000 years later.

The Camino makes its way towards Milladoiro jumping from short sections of dirt trails to country lanes and suburban residential areas as it avoids the busy N-550 to the right. The route is well marked and surprisingly peasant considering the distance from Santiago. There are, however, very few services for pilgrims.

O Milladoiro (Km 8.3)

O Milladoiro is your last hill on Camino and, despite the buildings, once you have left town you will get a glimpse of the city and the cathedral towers. This magical moment happens about half way down the hill after having left O Milladoiro.

Unfortunately, O Milladoiro is now a large suburb of Santiago with towering 15 story apartment blocks that provide affordable homes for young couples that work in Santiago, or larger homes with gardens for older couples that can afford them. The tiny baroque Chapel de la Magdalena feels almost out of place here and in my opinion is a sad reminder of bygone days.

However, despite its current appearance, O Milladoiro has always been associated with the Camino and has seen hundreds of thousands of pilgrims walk by. Even the name of the town appears to be linked to Camino tradition. *Milladoiro* derives from the Latin word *humillatorium*, which in Spanish is *humilladero* (a place where you *humble* yourself in English). In Spain, a *humilladero* is a place of religious significance, usually just before you enter a town, which usually displays a cross or another type of religious monument or image.

Thus, Santiago de Compostela's *humilladero* on the Portuguese Camino has always been O Milladoiro.

After O Milladoiro, you will be walking mostly downhill along small roads, through anodyne residential areas, through what's left of the village of A Rocha Vella and over a major expressway and the railway tracks. It's on this stretch, about halfway down the hill that you may see the cathedral for the first time!

A 10.000.000 euros (or more) theft

O Milladoiro is perhaps best known because of the headlines it made across the world, as it was here that the cathedral electrician, Mr. José Manuel Fernández lived and where the police eventually found in 2012 the stolen Códex Calixtinus that he had previously stolen from the cathedral's archives.

The priceless 12th century manuscript (valued in over 10 million euros) was found wrapped in a plastic bag in Mr. Fernández's garage a year later. In February 2015, Mr. Fernández was given a 10 year prison sentence and his wife and an accomplice, 6 months.

Santiago de Compostela city limits (Km 3 approx.)

Entering Santiago

The Camino between Milladoiro and the cathedral is well marked, even once you start walking on sidewalks. The Camino enters the historic quarter through the *Porta Faxeira* (don't look for a gate or door, it's just the name of the entrance to the old historic quarter), and then down *Rúa do Franco*, which flows into the *Praza do Obradoiro* and the cathedral.

Here are directions to get you to the cathedral:

Once you get to the bottom of the hill, you will cross the River Sar (more like a stream) over a quaint small bridge. The Camino makes its way through the woods till it passes under the major expressway that circles the city. Note that your last bar before the city is the quaint little Bar *A Paradiña* (translates as *The little stop* or *quick break*).The Camino then makes it way through the city suburbs until you are faced with the last dilemma of your Camino. **For reasons unknown to anyone but the** perpetrators, you will arrive to a small intersection with two milestones. The problem is that these milestones indicate opposite directions, one to the left and the other to the right.

You want to take the route to your LEFT, towards SANTA MARTA. The route to the right to CONXO is longer, makes no sense and does not pass by any landmark of interest.

Once you have turned to the left, the Camino soon becomes the main street into town, the one you will follow, in almost a straight line, to the *Porta Faxeira*, which begins as *Rúa Victor Muñoz* and ends as *Avenida Xoan Carlos I*, just before the historic quarter.

Facing the *Porta Faxeira* is the often-overlooked *Parque de Alameda* (for a stunning view of the cathedral, go to the viewpoint in the park). *Rúa do Franco* starts at *Porta Faxeira* and ends in the *Praza do Obradoiro*, which is the main square in front of the cathedral facing the *Pórtico de la Gloria* and the end of your Camino!

Statue of the 'Dos Marías' (Two Marys)

Just before you enter the historic quarter of Santiago through the Puerta Faxeiras, you will walk through or bypass the Alameda Park. Inside the park is one of the most singular and beloved statues in the city, the statue of the 'Dos Marías'.

The 'Dos Marías' were the sisters Maruxa and Coralia Fandiño, who lived in Santiago during the 20th century. They became well known and loved by the locals throughout the city because of their eccentric behaviour in the 1950s and 1960s. The sisters would go for a walk together every day at precisely two in the afternoon and flirt with the local university students. For these daily walks they would dress in what could be considered back then as inappropriate clothing and wear heavy make up. Surprisingly the very conservative religious and political authorities during the dictatorship tolerated the two sisters, probably considering them as harmless mentally disturbed ladies.

However, the story of the Dos Marías is not as bright as it may appear. Several of their brothers were members of the anarchist syndicate CNT and political activists prior to the Spanish Civil War. Once the war began, the nationalists in Santiago began the purge of any elements considered to be contrary to fascism and Franco's regime. On finding that the brothers had escaped and possibly fled the country, the sisters were detained for questioning, where they were tortured and raped. It is unclear whether or not the sisters had been involved in any sort of political activism prior to the war. After the war, the sisters and their mother were condemned to poverty and social exclusion, as it would have been dangerous for other locals to associate closely with them.

The question that remains was whether the sisters went crazy after their ordeal, or whether they were perfectly sane and this was the only way they found to confront the regime.

Santiago de Compostela

Santiago is a town you will immediately fall in love with. The historic quarter is small (but large enough to explore for several days), manageable and safe (no cars and very little crime if any). It has also been fairly untouched and when you walk through the streets and quiet alleys you may feel like you have been transported back in time. Indeed, when I was reading 19th century Bazán's *Pazos de Ulloa*, part of which takes place in Santiago, her descriptions fit like a glove to my own observations of the town, more than a hundred years later.

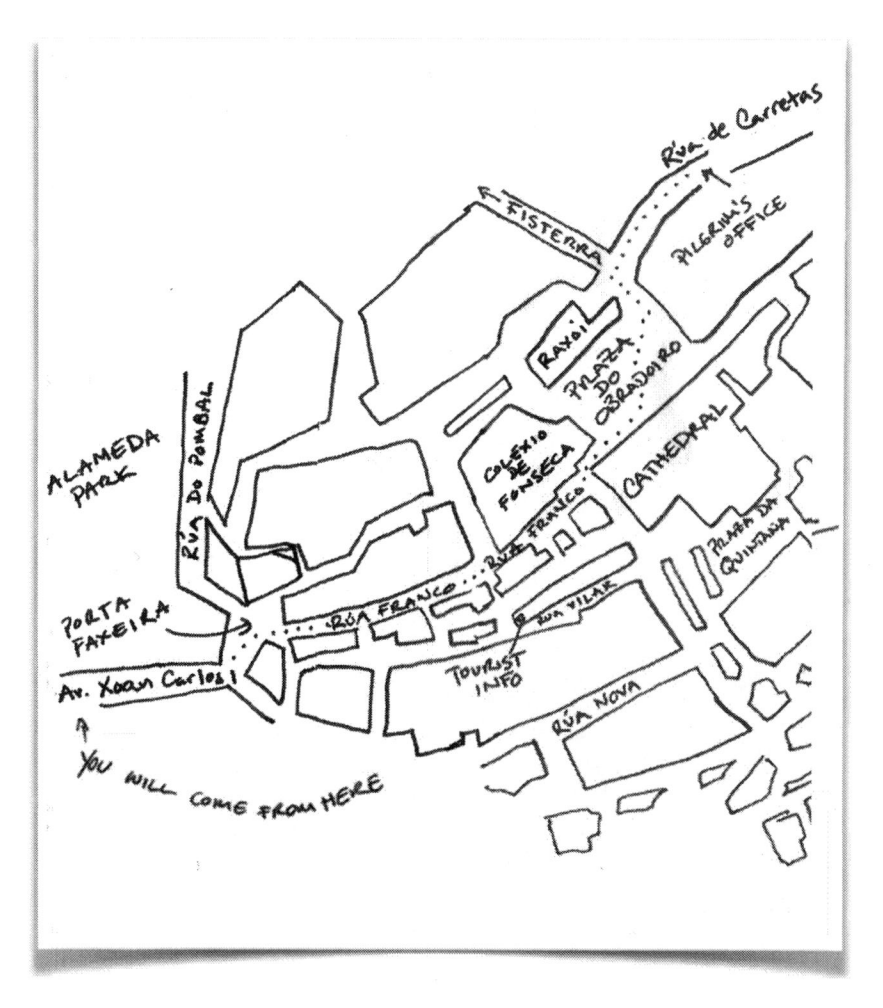

That said, Santiago is also a tourist town, it has been one for over a thousand years, and it has also strived and fed off of tourists and pilgrims for over a thousand years. Indeed, everything around you has probably come (one way or another) from a fellow pilgrim at some time in history. So don't be put off by all the souvenir shops, they've been around since Alfonso II built his first church; nor by all the restaurants and bars, they too have been around since then. Times may have changed but the essence of the journey and the needs of the traveller (pilgrim included) have not.

The historical accounts

Münzer arrived in Santiago in December 1494, describing the city as, "situated in the middle of a complete circle of mountains. In the middle is another hill, elevated as if it were raised up in the center of the circle. It has no river, but many and good fountains, that flow with sweet water. It is not big, but very old, and it is fortified with a very old wall and numerous and solid towers."

Regarding the cathedral, he says, 'The church of Santiago is one of the three principal ones, following in order that of Rome and that of Ephesus in Asia, which has just disappeared. It was built by Charlemagne, King of the Franks, and Emperor of Germany who, (...) paid for it with the spoils, donations and tribute of the Saracens.' For the record, we know for sure that Charlemagne did not build or contribute to the cathedral's construction. However, my favourite part of his account is his poor opinion of the pilgrims, describing their behavior as, 'so loud is the continual chatter in the Cathedral, that you would think you were at a fair. There is very little devotion there. The very holy Apostle should be shown more veneration'

Confalonieri arrived in spring, on May 4th of 1594 and his description of the city is similar to Münzer's. 'The city is small and it is on a sterile hill. In general in all of Galicia, and mostly in this area, is made up of hills, that are like waves of the sea, all barren, without a tree, or very few; however, this land is abundant with fresh water. This city is never hot, rather cold or mild than warm. It rains a lot.' He is also impressed by the university in town, describing it as having 'many students, dressed in yellow. Grammar, Rhetoric, Philosophy, Theology, Scholastics, Canons and Civil Law are read. The number of students – on the Feast of Saint Luke, when the courses begin after the August and September vacations – is 1200 or 1300, not more than 1400.'

Confalonieri also briefly describes the cathedral as, 'Above all is the notable and glorious church of Santiago, built in the shape of a cross. You enter through one of the side doors of the cross and not through the main one, in front of the main altar.' However, the Italian is a bit more interested in the pilgrim rites, which he describes in detail, 'Above (the altar) there is a statue of Santiago, of marble, painted, with the cross of Santiago on his chest, and on his head a hanging silver crown, and all the pilgrims that arrive here go up some steps behind the altar to hug and kiss the statue and put the crown on their heads.'

Rosmithal arrived in Santiago in 1467. His description of the city coincides with the other two pilgrims, 'The city of Santiago sits between large mountains, It's very spacious and its surrounded by a single wall, with towers, which can be seen from afar, and by walls covered with ivy that look like a forest; the city is surrounded by a wide moat and the walls are crowned by old square towers, that are close together.'

However, the Czech's account of Santiago is somewhat different as when Rosmithal and his party arrived to Santiago de Compostela they found a city in turmoil as the Archbishop Fonseca and several priests had been taken prisoner by the local Count of Trastamara. The Count was also laying siege to the cathedral where the archbishop's mother and brother were defending themselves. Unexpectedly, Rosmithal was able to maneuver around this awkward situation and gain access to the cathedral. Inside they were given a VIP tour of the treasures and were able to admire several relics, such as the axe that beheaded Santiago and the staff the saint carried on his pilgrimages.

Surprisingly, none of the three pilgrims mention the Pórtico de La Gloria in their accounts, which makes you wonder as this artistic masterpiece would have been there.

Santiago, UNESCO World Heritage Site

Indeed, the whole Camino de Santiago is also a World Heritage Site. However, the city of Santiago de Compostela also figures in its own right independently from the Camino. As the UNESCO site describes:

'Santiago de Compostela, owing to its monumental integrity, enshrines both specific and universal values. To the irreplaceable uniqueness of Romanesque and Baroque masterpieces is added the transcendental aesthetic contribution, which makes use of diachronic and disparate elements in the construction of an ideal city which is overflowing with history. The exemplary nature of this city of Christian pilgrimage which is enriched by the ideological connotations of the Reconquista is echoed by the great spiritual significance of one of the few places that are so deeply imbued with faith as to become sacred for the tile of humanity.'

Toponymy of Santiago de Compostela

The city is named after the Apostle *Santiago el Mayor* (St. James the Greater, not to be confused with his fellow Apostle St. James the Lesser). The city is named after St. James because this is the final resting place of his body. His remains can be found in the crypt of the cathedral. Tradition would like to believe that the name *Compostela* derives from the Latin words *Campus Stellae* (field of stars). However, it may also derive from the Latin words *Composita Tella* (burial ground). I like the first option better as it fits perfectly with the Camino myth and its symbolism.

I will conclude this guidebook with some useful information for the end of your pilgrimage, some final legends and stories associated with Santiago and some personal suggestions regarding the town and what it has to offer. In this manner I will try to enhance your visit to Santiago by providing information that you may not readily find elsewhere.

Further information on the churches, monasteries, convents and museums that you can visit in town is available online, at the tourist office (5-minute stroll from the cathedral on *Rúa do Vilar*).

Information on places to stay, eat and drink can also be found on a hundred websites (Everybody loves *Tripadvisor*). Consider booking in advance during the peak season (especially August).

Flashy colour tourist maps of the city are usually provided at hotels and hostels, or at the tourist office on *Rúa do Vilar*.

The last metres to the cathedral, the Praza de Obradoiro and the cathedral

The Avenida de Xoán Carlos I ends at the Porta Faxeira (The *Public* or *No Secrets* Gate), which is where the Porta Faxeira once stood, and that received the pilgrims entering the city as it still symbolically does to this day.

Once inside the 'walled' part of the city, pilgrims are a short stroll to the cathedral. Aymeric Picaud describes how these streets leading to the cathedral *'were packed with money-changers, innkeepers and merchants of all descriptions'* and how in the plaza in front of the north door to the cathedral (now known as Plaza de Azabachería), the locals would *'sell scallop shells to pilgrims... as well as wineskins, deerskin, knapsacks, bags, straps, belts and all sorts of medicinal herbs and other spices, and many other products besides.'*

Reading these descriptions from 800 years ago, one cannot but feel that things have not changed that much in Santiago de Compostela. Perhaps the merchants have become a bit more sophisticated, but their wares are uncannily similar.

The Fountain do Franco on Rúa do Franco

Right on Rúa do Franco and only a stone's throw away from the Cathedral is the usually overlooked Fountain do Franco.

Restored in 1830, tradition believes that it was here that the thirsty oxen that were transporting Saint James's corpse to his burial place stopped for a drink and a spring miraculously appeared where the desperate oxen started digging with their hooves. You have to love these stories.

Apparently, the water from the fountain has (or at least had) curative properties; Francis of Siena the Blessed was cured in the 13th century of his blindness after completing his pilgrimage to Santiago de Compostela.

The Praza do Obradoiro has unofficially become *Kilometre 0* for the thousands of pilgrims that complete their pilgrimage every year. The name of the plazas roughly translates as the *Workmen's Square*, and it was here that much of the action happened during the construction of the cathedral.

The Plaza is also flanked by some of the most important monuments in Santiago. As you face the Cathedral, to your left stands the Plateresque style (Spanish Renaissance) *Hostal de los Reyes Católicos*, that dates from 1492 and served as a pilgrims' hospice and later as a hospital all the way into the 20th century. It is now an exclusive hotel and no longer caters to pilgrims on a budget. Still facing the cathedral and to your back stands the *Palacio de Rajoy* dating from the 18th century. This building now houses the Town Hall. To your right is the *Colegio de San Colegio de San Jerónimo* from the 16th century, which is now the seat of the Rector of the University of Santiago. Finally, in front of you is the grandiose west façade of the cathedral, finished in Baroque style in 1750, and which covers the former medieval Romanesque façade.

The Plaza de Obradoiro continues to be the heart of the city, where pilgrims and tourists, students and professors, government and religious dignitaries, and buskers and drifters still mingle, 1200 years later.

Regarding the cathedral, the first chapel was built over the tomb of the Apostle in the early 9th century and was commissioned by Alfonso II the Chaste. This chapel was followed by another church in the early 10th century, which was razed by the Moors during an incursion. In 1075 work began on the present cathedral and the temple was consecrated in 1211. In this manner the interior of the cathedral is a progression of Romanesque styles and presents a classic layout for pilgrimage cathedrals: a Latin cross foundation shape, a three-aisled barrel vaulted nave, a gallery that runs around the whole building and an ambulatory that links the aisles behind the main altar. Aymeric Picaud describes the current cathedral as: *'In this church there is no fault; it is admirably constructed, large, spacious, light, with harmonious dimensions, well proportioned as to length, width and height; it is more splendid than words can express...'*

However, the architectural jewel of the cathedral is unquestionably the *Pórtico de la Gloria*, that is, the west Romanesque door that is now hidden by the west Baroque façade. This masterpiece is the work of *Master Mateo* and was completed in 1188. The *Pórtico de la Gloria* boasts over 200 sculpted figures that appear to almost come to life as they realistically interact amongst themselves. This kind of artistic representation was unheard of in the early Romanesque period and heralds the advent of the upcoming Gothic style. Be warned that in 2018 the *Pórtico de la Gloria* was reopened to the public and there were record queues to visit it, and it's not free.

Pilgrim rites

You have read about them, seen them in the films, and looked forward to this moment for days, weeks, perhaps months. Tradition says that there are three rites a pilgrim must do when he reaches the cathedral: a) place his or her hand on the column that holds Santiago in the Pórtico de la Gloria, b) place his or her forehead on Maestro Mateo's forehead, and c) go up behind the altar, touch (or hug) the statue of Santiago and then go below to the crypt where his bones rest in a cask.

Of these rites you can now only do the third one, that is, hug the saint and then visit the crypt for a quiet moment or to pray (if you feel inclined to). I assume that this is the price of fame, and that the corrosive sweat on our hands added to the sheer numbers of pilgrims (and tourists) who visit the cathedral has led the cathedral cabildo (council of canons) to protect these areas with methacrylate. Regarding the saint, I have not tried to put my pilgrim's hat or cloak on the saint (as they did back in the day), but I am pretty sure that the sour-faced guard on duty would not like it. He also gets very annoyed if you stop for pictures (remember, there may be a long queue behind you). Another thing that surprises most of the pilgrims in my groups is that you are actually up and behind the altar, so you are hugging Santiago from behind (makes sense as he is facing the nave).

And if you thought that all of this was disappointing, there is more. Pilgrims and tourists still have free access to the cathedral (Santiago is one of the few cathedrals that does not charge visitors in Spain), but not to the Cathedral Museum; however, pilgrims do get a two euro discount on your ticket if you can produce your pilgrim's credential (8 euros instead of 10!).

The rest of the cathedral can be visited (even the roof) and yes, your guidebooks and art books are right, it is a jewel of Romanesque art. Give yourself some time to explore and pilgrim watch from one of the pews.

Note: In 2022, because of Covid-19 safety measures, pilgrims were not allowed to touch (or hug) the statue of Saint James. This ban will probably continue until the end of the pandemic.

Your Compostela

You have walked it so you have earned it. The *Compostela* is requested at the brand new Pilgrim's Office, which is now around the corner from the cathedral, on *Rúa das Carretas*. Go down the steps at the far end of the Praza do Obradoiro and take the first right, that's *Rúa das Carretas*. Remember that up to 1500 pilgrims arrive every day and they all want their *Compostela* too! The wait isn't too bad as you will most likely run into friends or acquaintances made days before on the Camino, or perhaps make new ones and start telling each other Camino stories.

The *Compostela* is free and the office is usually manned (or *womanned*) by volunteers. However, you can leave a small donation. The office also sells for a euro a very handy small travel carton tubes for your *Compostela*.

The *Compostela* is a replicate of the century-old certificate that has been awarded to pilgrims since anyone can remember. It is written in Latin and you get your name translated into Latin too (unless it is a classic Latin or Catholic name you may just end up with a –us or -um at the end of it).

When you request it you will be asked to provide proof of your pilgrimage. This is when you produce your Pilgrim's Credential with all the stamps properly dated. The friendly people at the office will ask you where you started, where you are from and the reason for doing the pilgrimage, and anything else they feel like related to your pilgrimage.

The office awards a slightly different *Compostela* for those pilgrims that have walked the Camino for cultural reasons and not spiritual or religious ones; it is also in Latin but the layout is a bit different and you do not get the Saint's blessing. Likewise, you can also request a *Distance Certificate*, which is pretty, costs 3 euros, is written in Spanish and certifies who you are, where you started and how many kilometres you have walked.

The office is open until 9:00 pm from April to October (and Easter week), and until 7:00 the rest of the year.

Note: In 2021, a somewhat complex procedure for requesting you Compostela was launched. Pilgrims must first register on the Pilgrim Office website after which they will obtain a QR code, this is not optional. With this code they must go to the Pilgrim Office basement and request a number for the queue. Without the QR code, the staff in the basement will not provide you with a number to join the queue. Once you have your number for the queue, which will also have another QR code, you can check the approximate waiting time online and/or join the queue. Numbers are displayed on a monitor in the hall. Depending on the season, expect to wait a bit or not get a number at all for that day (in summer, queue numbers may run out for the day by midday).

Link to register:
https://catedral.df-server.info/agencias/Banderas.aspx?ind=1

Pilgrim's Mass

The Pilgrim's Mass is celebrated daily at noon. And no, you will most likely not see the *botafumeiro*. It is a Catholic Mass, celebrated in Spanish at the end of which a general pilgrim's blessing is given and the nationalities of the different pilgrims that arrived the previous day are called out. Get there early if you intend to sit.

The cathedral also offers confession before the Mass in several languages.

Vespers (evening prayer and Mass in Spanish) are nice, less crowded and take place daily at 7:30 pm.

I have also discovered thanks to a pilgrim in one of my groups that if you are a (Catholic) priest and a pilgrim (and have brought the necessary paperwork from home), it is possible to co-officiate the Pilgrim's Mass. In fact, it is not unusual to see a group of priests up on the altar with the local priest officiating the Mass.

Botafumeiro

That's the large not-quite-silver incense burner (censer) that is swung along the transept of the church (not the nave, so if you happen to be in town when they are going to swing it, don't sit in the nave). It is swung on major religious festivals (not necessarily Sundays) and other Masses, prior request and a 400 euro donation (this was in 2019) to the cathedral; and sorry, no matter what you have heard, the *botafumeiro* is no longer swung at Friday evening Mass.

The origin of the *botafumeiro* can most likely be found in the need to mask the smell of hundreds of pilgrims (many would have even slept in the cathedral) during medieval times. A large pilgrimage centre such as Santiago required a very large incense burner, and a large cathedral such as Santiago required swinging it as far as possible to reach the whole church.

Indulgences

If you are in Santiago de Compostela (not necessarily walking), you can claim plenary or partial indulgence.

Plenary indulgence is the concession by the Catholic Church of the full temporal remission of a person's sins. Plenary indulgence is obtained if, once in Santiago, you also find time to pray, confess, attend Mass and take communion. But before you consider engaging in any sinful behaviours, keep in mind that plenary indulgence is only granted on holy years or on a series of meaningful dates on normal years (eg. the 25th of July).

If you are in Santiago and it is not a holy year, you can claim partial indulgence. This basically means that a part of your temporal sins are remitted. The percentage or number of your sins forgiven is not disclosed. The procedure is the same as in plenary indulgence.

The Catholic Church has definitely come a long way since the Middle Ages (and later) when indulgences were sold and bought as stock market shares (their value being the number of days on Earth or in the Purgatory forgiven for your sins). Apparently, it was not until Vatican II when the pope clarified that the days of pardon stated in partial indulgences did not refer to our days on earth but rather to more abstract periods of celestial time.

In any case, after having been (and as a quasi-pilgrim in most cases) to Santiago more than 10 times, I am pretty sure I have been pardoned some of my lesser sins.

Holy Year

That's when the 25th of July falls on a Sunday. The 2021 Holy Year was extended to 2022 for the first in Camino history. The next one will be in 2027.

Thank you, Pope Francis!

Santiago el Mayor (St. James the Greater)

St. James the Greater was one of Christ's apostles and in line with instructions received at Pentecost, he set out to preach in Hispania (current day Iberian Peninsula). He did a very poor job of it and returned to Palestine. One thing led to another and he ended up martyred by beheading by king Herod in Jerusalem, thus becoming the first apostle martyred.

The Virgin Mary and St. James

Tradition says that the Virgin Mary played a significant role in one of the major events in St. James's life. This occurred while he was preaching, somewhat disheartened, on the banks of the Ebro river in Hispania. The Virgin appeared to him mounted on a column and ordered him to build a church in her honour. A small church was built by St. James, becoming the first church to be erected in honour of the Virgin Mary. Tradition also says that the column that is conserved in the Basilica of Our Lady in the Spanish city of Zaragoza (the place of the miracle) is the original one from the story. Two main Spanish national holidays are the 25th of July (Festivity of Santiago and patron saint of Spain) and the 12th of October (Festivity of Our Lady of the Pilar).

Legend of the remains and burial of Santiago

After Santiago was martyred in Jerusalem, his followers managed to smuggle his body out of Palestine, load it on a boat made of stone, without a crew, and without sails that sailed all the way to the town of Iria Flavia (current day Padrón) on the western Galician coast. In other words, his body was taken back to Hispania. His followers buried him near there and the location was forgotten until the year 813 when the hermit Pelayo saw strange lights and heard celestial music coming from a hill (the Campus Stellae or field of stars). The local bishop Teodomiro was sought and a marble coffin was found with the name of Santiago inscribed on it. The local king was also notified (Alfonso II) and a church was built.

The Codex Calixtinus elaborates on this legend adding the following story: When Santiago's followers took his body off the boat that had brought them from Palestine, they entered the dominions of (legendary) Queen Lupa. The followers requested two oxen to transport the body and a place to bury Santiago. The Queen sent them to a nearby hill guarded by a dragon to collect the oxen (in reality two wild bulls). Just before they were devoured by the dragon, their prayers were answered and they were saved, the dragon killed and the wild bulls domesticated. The Queen, impressed by the miracle, converted to Christianity and provided a burial place.

Santiago's bones, however, had not finished their pilgrimage. Several times during the next centuries the bones were hidden in the event of foreign invasions. It was in one of these incursions, the possibility of a raid in 1589 by Sir Francis Drake, that the bones were hidden so well that they were lost for 300 years. In 1879 his bones were found (under the cathedral) and later authenticated by the Pope Leo XII.

Legend of the battle of Clavijo

This is perhaps Santiago's best and most controversial miracle. During a decisive battle between Ramiro I (Christian king) and Abderramán II (Muslim king) in 844 near the town of Clavijo, Santiago himself decided to appear mounted on a white horse, sword in hand, and help the Christians win the day just when they were about to be defeated. The battle was apparently fought when the Christian king decided he would no longer pay the tribute of 100 maidens to the Muslims. Enthusiasts consider this battle a turning point in the Christian reconquering effort, and to an extent it was as a powerful symbol was found to unite Christian forces against a common enemy. Unfortunately, historic revision seriously questions the authenticity of the battle (whether or not Santiago appeared is up to you).

The image of Santiago, patron of Spain, on a white horse wielding his sword and striking down several Muslims can be found in churches through out Spain and any country that was a previous Spanish colony. This powerful image would come to represent Spanish pride and nationalism against any foreign aggression. Unsurprisingly, Franco's fascist troops also considered Santiago to be on their side during the Spanish Civil War.

Tribute of the 100 maidens

In 783, the Christian king Mauregato rose to the throne with the aid of the Muslim king Abderramán I. Part of the tributes that Mauregato was required to pay the Muslim Emirate were 100 maidens. The tribute was eventually changed for a money tribute, which in turn was rejected by Alfonso II in 794. Fifty years later, Abderramán II attempted to impose the tribute of 100 maidens again and was defeated in the Battle of Clavijo.

Some things I like to do in Santiago

Eating with the locals

I have only good things to say about the following restaurants in Santiago. Restaurant *Dezaseis* on *Rúa de San Pedro* next to the *Porta do Camiño* is a long-time favourite in many guidebooks, which explains the presence of other tourists and pilgrims. But the food and service are excellent and the prices more than reasonable. Restaurant *As Hortas* faces the well-known Michelin star *Casa Marcelo*, serves fresh produce, fine dining and less hype than its neighbour. For another Michelin Star experience, *A Tafona* on *Rúa da Virxe da Cerca* delivers (and you deliver your credit card). *A Curtidoría* around the corner from the Cathedral makes for a memorable evening if it's tablecloths and fine service you are after. Finally, the down to earth and very affordable *Casa Manolo* on *Praza Cervantes* is considered a Camino institution by the pilgrim community. It was here that I celebrated my first Camino over 20 years ago!

The *Abastos* market is also a great place to grab a bite. Just buy your seafood fresh from one of the stalls and then for a small fee ask the small bar in the market to prepare it for you for lunch!

For the record, I usually stay off the restaurants on *Rúa do Franco*, nothing wrong with them, just too many tourists.

> **Abastos market**
>
> *This is the local market found within the old city, facing the street Virxe de la Cerca. It is a great place to wander around in the early morning when the locals are doing their shopping, or even before, when the stalls are opening and the fresh produce (fish, meat, vegetables…) is coming in for the day's sales. You will even see local farmers from outside of the city lay out their veggies on the ground around the market area. It is perhaps one of the few markets left that, although immersed in a tourist city, still maintains its local and authentic nature.*

Drinking with the locals

Santiago is full of places to get a drink, whether a *café con leche* in the morning, an *albariño* in the afternoon, or a *gin and tonic* in the evening. Rather than recommend a place, it's much more fun to wander around, peek inside and try one (or two) out. Places are all pretty much the same (either a cafeteria type setting or a bar setting) and prices will not vary significantly.

Remember that in Spain cafeterias serve alcohol and bars also serve coffee. However, locals tend to gravitate to a bar or pub setting towards the evening as the tapas are better and the ambience is more geared towards having a drink (or two). There are very few *local* bars left in the historic quarter; those are the ones that look dodgy, have no pretensions and are full of middle-aged or elderly Spanish males (you won't usually see women). Most tourists avoid these places and the bar is not worried about adding tourists to its clientele.

Santiago is a tapas city, that is, they do tapas the right way (in my book the right way is the *free way*). You can also order food at any bar, but I would suggest that before ordering food (and after ordering your drinks), wait a bit and see if a freebie comes with it. Not everyone does free tapas (even less on the *Rúa do Franco*), but enough do, and some of the free tapas are really good! And if you see everyone is getting a free tapa (it will be roughly the same one for everyone) and you don't have one, don't be shy, ask for it.

Gin and tonics in Galicia (and Spain)

Spaniards, who have traditionally shunned gin, have gone crazy with the stuff. Gin and tonics are in fashion and ordering one now bequeaths you with an aureole of glamour. But ordering a gin and tonic is no longer as simple as it was. Bars and pubs may now stock up to 15 types of gins and may even ask you what tonic you want. Then it's lime, or lemon, or cucumber, or rose petals, or sloe, or whatever the bartender feels the drink requires so as to enhance its taste. My personal theory is that half of Spain has read Fifty Shades of Grey, and Mr. Grey drinks gin and tonics.

If you want to show off with your foreigner friends and impress the locals, ask for Nordes gin. It's a locally produced gin, which you will either love or hate.

Museums and other sights

There are dozens of different museums, art galleries, convents, monasteries and churches that can be visited. The tourist office (*Rúa do Vilar*) is a great place to go for information; or, if you would rather surf the web, the Santiago tourist information website is quality: www.santiagoturismo.com, and in English!

Apart from the cathedral itself, you may want to consider visiting the recently inaugurated *Museo das Peregrinacións* (Pilgrimage Museum) at *Praza de Praterías*, as you will most likely relate to most of what's exhibited there.

Shopping

Santiago has it all, from top designers and fashion stores around the *Praza de Galicia* (just off the historic quarter), to trinkets and dodgy souvenirs spread out in the historic quarter. Prices will not vary and pretty much everyone is selling the same stuff. There are some exceptions though.

For souvenirs or just items of a religious nature, have a look around the shops just off the *Praza da Quintana* and the *Rúa de Fonseca* (next to the cathedral near the pilgrim's office). For upscale expensive ceramics and pottery, have a look in *Sargadellos* on *Rúa Nova*. For fantastic scallop shell shaped knockers or just embellishments for your gate or door, any of the hardware stores around town. And for jewellery, I go to *Maeloc*, which is the large store right next to the cathedral, on *Rúa do Franco*. Obviously, I tend to gravitate around the *Abastos* market for my cheese and sometimes my wine.

Leaving Santiago

Most pilgrims leave Santiago by plane, train or bus. Rental cars are also typically picked up at the airport, although there are agencies in Santiago city.

Getting to the airport

Take a cab for a flat fare of 22 euros (in 2022) and it's a 20-30 minute drive from the city centre to the airport. Or jump on the airport bus from *Praza de* Galicia (in front of the Hotel Husa) for 3 euros (every half an hour) and it will take 30-40 minutes. Airport in Spanish is *Aeropuerto*. Look out for the milestones inside the airport, there is one at *Departures*!

Santiago is an international airport, with flights abroad. Apart from *IBERIA*, the Spanish national airline, there are also budget airlines (usually a cheaper option if you do not have a lot of luggage and buy in advance) that fly to Madrid, Barcelona and a handful of other cities, such as *Vueling* and *Ryanair*. Budget airlines require purchasing tickets online and printing your boarding pass before going to the airport (if you forget to do this, it will cost you you dearly!).

Surprisingly, Santiago de Compostela is not well connected with Lisbon or Porto in Portugal by air or by train.

Getting to the train station (Avenida de Lugo)

A cab will get you there in 10 minutes for under 10 euros. There are several local buses that will also take you there, but be warned that the bus service in Santiago is infrequent and not easy to use if you are not a local. It could even be walking distance if your hotel is in that direction and you don't have a heavy bag. Train station in Spanish is *Estación de tren*.

Spain only operates one national rail company: RENFE. The information desks are helpful and speak English. However, most people buy their tickets online before travelling, printing off their ticket at home or hotel.

Getting to the bus station (Avenida de Rodríguez de Viguiri)

The brand-new bus station is next to the train station. Bus station in Spanish is *Estación de bus*. Bus station in Spanish is *Estación de bus*.

There are several companies operating in the terminal. However, if you are on a long distance trip, you will most likely be on an ALSA bus. Tickets can be purchased online or at the station.

So you made it, you've done the rites, got your *Compostela*, taken off your pilgrim gear and are now a tourist again; and now what?

Having completed your Camino and once you have been transformed back into a tourist, it's time to consider options for the time you have in Santiago.

Option 1: Continue walking

Get your gear back on and before you have second thoughts, get on the Camino again to Finisterre, to see the *end of the world*. You leave town from the Praza do Obradoiro, opposite the cathedral.

Option 2: Visit some of the surrounding towns

Finisterre and Muxía

If you have decided that you have done your share of walking but still want to see Finisterre and jump into the ocean there, you can schedule a daytrip with one of the many tour companies that organise this excursion from Santiago. The daytrip will usually include the lovely town of Muxía too. Information on companies can be found at the tour office, at your hotel or on the Internet.

There is really nothing to see in Finisterre town. You will most likely head up to the lighthouse some kilometres out of town to catch the views from there as you will be standing on the most western point of continental Europe (I do not care what the Portuguese say about this not being true). Muxía, on the contrary, is a lovely small coastal town that has maintained some of its historic flavour and is also part of the Camino de Santiago. Just out outside of town and facing the sea is the spectacular *Santuario da Virxe da Barca* (Sanctuary of the Virgin of the Boat; the large rocks in front of the church are reputedly the remains of a stone boat).

A Coruña

The second largest city in Galicia and over double the size of Santiago, the city is an interesting melange of a busy port city and a quaint historic quarter equipped with a beautiful sandy beach. A Coruña is also one of the starting places for pilgrims walking the English Way (*Camino Inglés*). There is also a UNESCO World heritage site to be visited: A Roman lighthouse called the Tower of Hercules that is credited to have worked continuously for over 1800 years. There are frequent commuter trains and buses that will get you there in around 30 minutes from Santiago. A Coruña is north of Santiago, right on the coast.

Option 3: Chill in Santiago

This one warrants no explanation.

To conclude all I have left to do is to wish you a *Buen Camino*!

(or *Bom Caminho!*)

Annex I - Valença do Minho

Although this guidebook covers only the Spanish section of the Portuguese Camino to Santiago, I have decided to include a short chapter on Valença do Minho as many pilgrims that start in Tui consider crossing the river into Portugal and visiting this amazing fortified medieval city. Remember to set your watch back an hour if you do go, Portugal is an hour behind of Spain! Thankfully, both countries use the same currency, the euro.

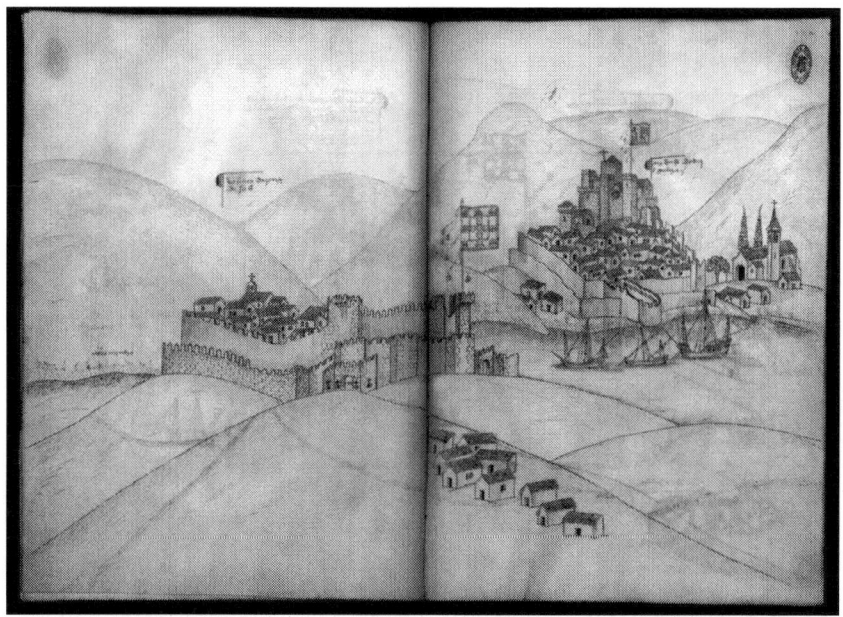

Illustration of Valença do Minho (on the left) and Tui (on the right). *Livro das Fortalezas*, 1509. Duarte de Armas, *Arquivo Nacional Torre do Tombo*. Creative Commons content.

Crossing the border

The Camino makes its way out of the Valença do Minho walled city through a rather inconspicuous archway in the medieval wall, and then down a ramp that leads you down to the International Bridge and the River Miño (See Stage 1 for more information on the bridge).

The River Miño is the international border between Portugal and Spain. There is no longer an immigration or customs post on either side of the border since 1995, when the Schengen Agreement amongst several European Union states became effective. This means that to cross the border you simply cross the bridge and continue your Camino. This Schengen Agreement also means that you cannot get a Portuguese or Spanish immigration stamp for your 'real' passport.

Toponomy of Valença do Minho

Like every other city named Valença or Valencia on the Iberian Peninsula, Valença do Minho was founded by the Romans. The name comes from the Latin word *'valentia'*, which translates as vigour, strength or courage. The Romans may have named these cities believing that they were actually naming the city after Rome, which was incorrectly (at the time) believed to have come from the Greek word for vigour, strength and courage. However, Valença was called *Contrasta* until the 13th century, when it was then renamed *Valença*.

So what is not clear is whether the supposed old Roman name of *'Valentia'* was recovered, or whether the city was simply renamed *Valença* referring to its *courage*. The 'do Minho' part is simple, it means 'of the Minho'. The Minho is the river you will cross, and which becomes the Miño in Spain.

The Miño/Minho River

The Miño (or Minho in Portugal) is Galicia's longest and largest river, running 350 kilometres southwest from central Galicia to the Atlantic Ocean where it becomes the natural border between Portugal and Spain. In this manner, the Miño crosses both the Portuguese Camino and the French Camino.

Look out for the legendary amphibian-mermaids as you cross the river. These mythological creatures called *xacias* have the bad habit of falling in love with humans and then marrying them. Be warned that these liaisons usually have sad endings.

An abbreviated history of Valença do Minho

Valença do Minho was founded by the Romans, although there was most likely a Celtic settlement here prior to their arrival. The city sits right on the Roman *Vía XIX* that you will be following all the way to Santiago de Compostela (look out for the Roman milestone right in the middle of the walled city). Like the rest of the region, Valença was only conquered and occupied by the Musilms for a relatively short span of time in the 8th century, although it continued to suffer successive Muslim assaults and sackings throughout the Middle Ages and until the Muslim threat to the Christian kingdoms in the north was neutralised. Then, the city would play a decisive role in maintaining the belligerent Spaniards on the other side of the river at bay after the expulsion of the Muslim kingdoms from this part of the Iberian Peninsula. The current (although somewhat altered) walls of the fortified city were built in the 13th century when the only real enemy in the region was Spanish and sitting across the river. The city would be occupied one last time by a foreign army during the Napoleonic wars in the 19th century.

The modern city

It is unlikely you will make it as far as the modern city if you have walked over from Spain for a day trip. The modern sprawl spreads south of the historic walled city and, although pleasant enough, offers little in the way of sightseeing. Lunches, however, will be much cheaper here than inside the fortified city, so perhaps it is worth the effort. The Camino enters the modern city and its suburbs from the south, makes its way up the busy *Avenida de Miguel Dantes* to a large roundabout where it then makes its way up into the walled city at the top of the small hill.

> San Teotonio (Saint Theotonius)
>
> Saint Theotonius is best known not because of his unusual name but because he is credited for being the first Portuguese saint.
>
> He was born just next door to Valença in the 11th century and lived to the ripe age of 84, when he passed away in Coimbra. During his life, the humble Theotonius refused to go beyond the title of prior, rejecting bishoprics and other honours, went on pilgrimage twice to the Holy Land (but not once to Santiago de Compostela), and served as counsellor and confessor to the first king of Portugal, Alfonso I.
>
> There is a statue commemorating Saint Theotonius inside the walled city.

The Fortress

The fortress and its walls require at least a couple of hours to explore and get a full picture of the historic medieval city. The current walls were altered in the 17th century so as to meet military standards of that epoch, mainly by adding bulwarks for cannons. The walled city is made up of two connected parts sitting on two separate small hills. Surrounding the whole fortress is a dry defensive moat.

The town within the walls resembles a classic Portuguese 18th and 19th century town, with white washed walls, cobblestone streets and a handful of reconstructed and/or renovated churches. Valença do Minho is a hugely popular tourist town, so expect crowds during the summer months. Also expect large sections of the historic quarter to be geared to the tourist crowds, with cafés, restaurants and tourist shops lining the streets and squares.

Interestingly, Valença has not quite shaken off the association Spain has of Portugal regarding bed linen and towels. For years, Spaniards have made a point out of crossing the border into Portugal to purchase these items as they were cheaper here than back home. This odd 70s heritage has persisted and is the reason you possibly see more shops in town selling towels, tablecloths and bed sheets than the usual knickknacks found in most tourist towns. So if you are looking for a beach towel figuring local soccer hero Cristiano Ronaldo, you just might be in luck.

The Rooster of Barcelos

The unofficial symbol of Portugal is without doubt the Rooster of Barcelos. In case you haven't run into it yet, it's the brightly coloured rooster motif you will see at any tourist shop in Portugal. What most tourists do not know is that the Rooster of Barcelos is part of a Camino story and one of its better-known legends. There is even a similar legend in Spain, although clearly the cultural impact was less.

The story goes as follows:

Once upon a time there was a pilgrim who was passing through the town of Barcelos. Barcelos is in northern Portugal and on the Camino. The pilgrim was unjustly accused of stealing some silver items from a wealthy landowner and sentenced to death. Before being hanged, the pilgrim asked to see the magistrate and plead his case. The locals agreed and took him before the magistrate who was just about to start his lunch of roasted chicken. The pilgrim, pointing to the rooster, said that it would crow at the moment he was hanged, proving his innocence. The magistrate ignored him but decided to leave his lunch untouched. The pilgrim was taken to the gallows and as he was being hung the rooster got up and crowed, which basically scared the pants off of everyone present. The magistrate, realising his error, ran to the save the pilgrim who luckily had already been spared by divine intervention. With a pat on the back and a huge sense of relief, the magistrate and locals sent the pilgrim on his way.

And the thief was never found.

Annex II - General Spanish etiquette

Picking/stealing farm food

You will be walking through a lot of farmland, sometimes literally next to the farmer's vegetable plots. If you and another 300.000 pilgrims each pick some grapes, corn or whatever, it won't be nice. Please be considerate when on the Camino, times have changed and gone are the days of free pickings and freebies.

Using rural toilets

What goes in must come out, and the bushes are full of pilgrims using the toilet. Once again, please be considerate and whatever you take into the bushes, bring it out with you and dispose of it where appropriate. I have seen some pretty nasty things in the bushes, which is absolutely uncalled for.

Graffiti on the Camino

I have mixed opinions on this one. On the one hand, I have read some particularly interesting and motivational graffiti, especially on the walls of the underpasses. I even have a photographic collection of the graffiti I have enjoyed the most (there's a wonderful snake telling pilgrims to call a taxi leaving Melide). Or another one in the underpass before Pedrouzo (Stage 7) with a quote by Dr. Seuss:

Be who you are and say what you feel, because those who mind don't matter and those who matter don't mind.

However, graffiti on milestones and on nature tends to be plain ugly. If you really need to write something or express yourself, consider chalk.

Rude waiters

Waiters at restaurants and bars in Spain are dry. They may or may not greet you, do not expect *you* to say *please*, will never say *you're welcome* and at times you will feel as if he or she has literally done you a favour by serving your food or drink. I am exaggerating, it isn't always this bad, but their mannerisms are most likely very different to what you are used to. For the record, don't ever think the manager will side with you if you are not satisfied with the service.

There are official complaint sheets at every business in Spain and you have the right to ask for them, and the bar must have them (if not, you are entitled to call the cops). I doubt there is much of a follow up of these sheets by the local authorities, but at least you annoy the owner.

Shoes and shirts

Please always wear a shirt and shoes (sandals are OK too, you are a pilgrim) when in a restaurant or bar. Spaniards really frown at shirtless barefoot people, no matter how warm it is. On the Camino, people are very tolerant to dust and mud, even the top end hotels you may stay at.

Smoking

Smoking is forbidden in any closed public space. However, Spaniards smoke and are very tolerant with smokers even if they don't smoke. They will get very confused if you get annoyed because someone is smoking outdoors, even at the terrace of a bar, and his/her smoke goes your way. Usually a polite request for him or her to be more careful and a smile will sort the matter out.

Paying and sharing bills

As a rule, Spaniards do not divide bills when paying, but divide equally amongst those present. They find it very odd that the rest of the world pays individually, even pulling out a calculator for extra precision. If you are with a group of Spaniards, you will most likely find yourself in this situation. So unless you had a coffee and the rest had two mixed drinks each, my recommendation is to go with the flow (Spanish etiquette would not allow the group to allow you to pay as much as them, everyone is aware of what's going on). It would also be considered very odd if at a lunch you insisted on calculating the exact amount you have spent when the group is dividing equally the meal (once again, if there are big differences, the Spaniards will be the first to sort this out).

Spaniards like to invite people to drinks, and everyone likes to have his or her drink paid for. However, if you have been invited to a drink, it is expected that when you have a chance, return the invitation (you will have to have another drink with him or her). Yes, we do keep a mental tally of all of this.

Tipping

Tipping may also be somewhat different than what you are used to. Remember that waiters make minimum wage, just like an office clerk, and although they work long hard hours, they are entitled to the same vacations as the rest of Spanish employees. In other words, at a bar, it is not unusual to not leave a tip at all. Usually it's the small change that you leave. At a restaurant you may leave between 5 and 10 percent, but only if you enjoyed the service. If you don't tip, no one is going to chase you into the street demanding it.

Kissing

We kiss when we greet each other or say good-bye. Two *air kisses* on both cheeks if it's two women or a woman and a man. Men shake hands unless they are family, in which case they may kiss as well. You may find yourself in a *kissing* situation, it's easy, wait for the local to approach you first, and then it's two air kisses on each cheek or a firm hand shake. Spaniards do not usually hug outside of their family.

Annex III - Accommodation

The following is a list of the public and some of the private hostels on the Camino. Expect to pay anywhere between 5 and 15 euros for a shared dorm and bathroom. Some hostels might include a simple continental breakfast. Likewise, opening times and dates differ significantly for each hostel. Finally, remember that the public hostels require a valid pilgrim credential to stay the night and you cannot make a reservation.

This is not a complete list of all the available hostels or accommodation options.

Tui

Albergue de Tui (public). Rúa Párroco Rodríguez Vázquez, s/n Tui. 40 beds.

Albergue el Camino (private). C/ Obispo Lago, 5. Tui. 24 beds.

Albergue Villa San Clemente (private). C/ Canónigo Valiño, 23. Tui. 27 beds.

Porriño

Albergue de O Porriño (public). Finca Isla. O Porriño. 52 beds.

Mos

Albergue de Santa Baia de Mos (public). Santa Eulalia, s/n. Mos. 16 beds.

Albergue de Peregrinos Santa Ana de Veigadaña (public). Petelos-Mos. 16 beds.

Redondela

Albergue de Casa da Torre de Redondela (public). Praza de Ribadavia, s/n. Redondela. 34 beds.

Albergue A Casa da Herba de Redondela (private). Praza de Alhóndiga. Redondela. 24 beds.

Albergue el Camino (private). C/ Telmo Bernárdez, 11. Redondela. 24 beds.

Pontevedra

Albergue de Pontevedra La Virgen Peregrina (public). Rúa Otero Pedrayo, s/n. 56 beds.

Albergue Aloxa Hostel (private). C/ Gorgullón, s/n. Pontevedra. 56 beds.

Slow City Hostel (private). Rúa da Amargura 5, 1º Izda. Pontevedra. 10 beds.

Briallos

Albergue de Briallos (public). Lugar de Castro e San Roque, s/n – Briallos. Portas. 27 beds.

Tivo

Albergue Turístico Catro Canos (private). Tivo, 58. Caldas de Reis. 18 beds.

Caldas de Reis

Albergue Posada Doña Urraca (public). C/ Campo de la Torre, 1. Caldas de Reis. 50 beds.

Albergue O Cruceiro (private). C/ Juan Fuentes, 44. Caldas de Reis. 38 beds.

Albergue Timonel (private). Travesía de las Ovejas, 8. Caldas de Reis. 18 beds.

Valga

Albergue de Valga (public). O Pino, Setecoros – Valga. 78 beds.

Pontecesures

Albergue de Pontecesures (public). Estrada das Escolas - Rúa Pousa Antelo. Infesta – Pontecesures. 52 beds.

Hospital de Peregrinos de Herbón (private). Monasterio de Herbón, s/n. Hebrón. Near Pontecesures. 20 beds.

Padrón

Albergue de Padrón (public). Costiña do Carme, s/n. Padrón. 48 beds.

Albergue Flavia (private). Campo da Feira, 13. Padrón. 22 beds.

Albergue Corredoiras (private). Corredoira da Barca, 10. Padrón. 26 beds.

Rúa de Francos

Albergue de Teo (public). Vilares de Rúa de Francos, s/n - Calo

Teo. 28 beds.

Regarding hotels, websites such as **www.booking.com**, **www.tripadvisor.com** or the Galician tourist board website, **www.turgalicia.es**, provide up to date information of all the major towns on the Camino as well as allowing booking in advance.

The author of *A Survival Guide to the Camino in Galicia* at a café in Palas de Rei on the French Camino, October 2023.

Jeffery Barrera currently works as a guide on both the Portuguese and French Caminos de Santiago. Since 2013 he has walked the Galician section of the Camino 75 times; in 1994 he walked to Santiago de Compostela from the French border and in 2019 he walked the Camino de Madrid. Because he gets to walk the Camino on a regular basis, he does not have to rely on other people for updates.

Jeffery Barrera is also the author of *A Survival Guide to the Portuguese Camino in Galicia* and *A Survival Guide to the Prado Museum*. Please visit **www.barrerabooks.com** for information about the author and his books.

Also by Jeffery Barrera

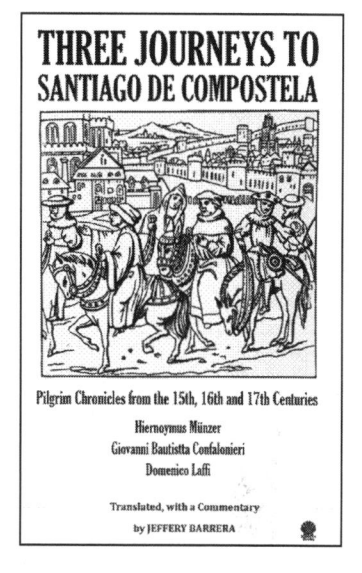

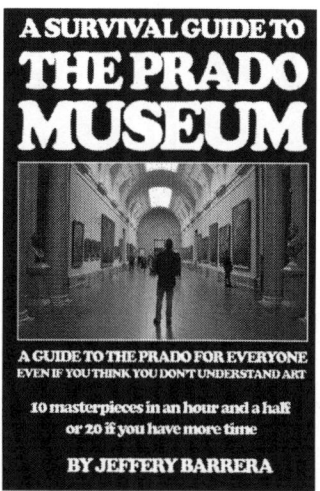

Available at www.barrerabooks.com

Made in the USA
Columbia, SC
04 March 2024